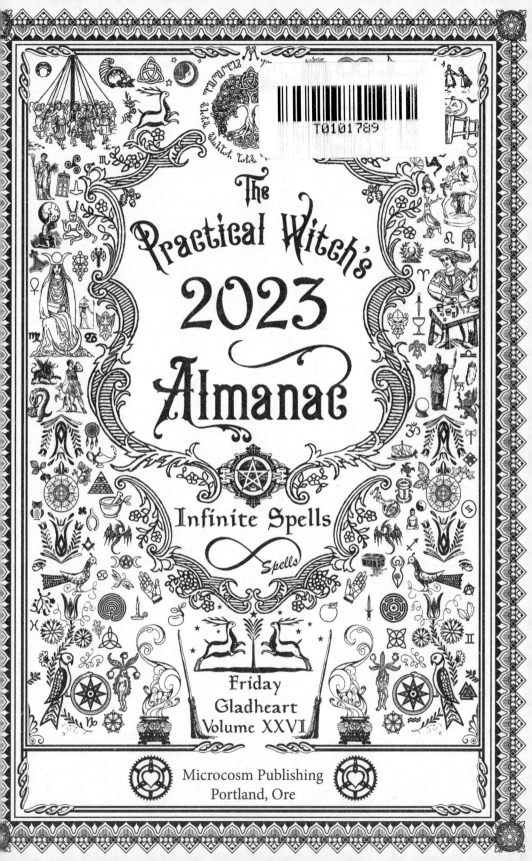

The Practical Witch's

2023

Almanac

Infinite Spells

Spells

Friday
Gladheart
Volume XXVI

Microcosm Publishing
Portland, Ore

T0101789

PRACTICAL WITCH'S ALMANAC 2023:
INFINITE SPELLS
© 2022 Friday Gladheart
© This edition Microcosm Publishing 2022
First edition
ISBN 978-1648411144

To join the ranks of high-class stores that feature Microcosm titles, talk to your local rep: In the U.S. **COMO** (Atlantic), **FUJII** (Midwest), **BOOK TRAVELERS WEST** (Pacific), **TURN-AROUND** (Europe), **UTP/MANDA** (Canada), **NEW SOUTH** (Australia/New Zealand), **GPS** in Asia, Africa, India, South America, and other countries, or **FAIRE** in the gift market.

For a catalog, write or visit:
Microcosm Publishing
2752 N Williams Ave.
Portland, OR 97227
https://microcosm.pub/PracticalWitch

The data in this almanac is calculated for Central Time. It is easy to convert the data to any time zone with the information on pages 8 and 9.

The Practical Witch's Almanac

2023 Edition: Volume XXVI
by Friday Gladheart

2023

January

M	T	W	T	F	S	S
						1
2	3	4	5	⑥	7	8
9	10	11	12	13	14	15
16	17	18	19	20	**21**	22
23	24	25	26	27	28	29
30	31					

February

M	T	W	T	F	S	S
		1	2	3	4	⑤
6	7	8	9	10	11	12
13	14	15	16	17	18	19
20	21	22	23	24	25	26
27	28					

May

M	T	W	T	F	S	S
1	2	3	4	⑤	6	7
8	9	10	11	12	13	14
15	16	17	18	**19**	20	21
22	23	24	25	26	27	28
29	30	31				

June

M	T	W	T	F	S	S
			1	2	③	4
5	6	7	8	9	10	11
12	13	14	15	16	**17**	18
19	20	21	22	23	24	25
26	27	28	29	30		

September

M	T	W	T	F	S	S
				1	2	3
4	5	6	7	8	9	10
11	12	13	**14**	15	16	17
18	19	20	21	22	23	24
25	26	27	28	㉙	30	

October

M	T	W	T	F	S	S
						1
2	3	4	5	6	7	8
9	10	11	12	13	**14**	15
16	17	18	19	20	21	22
23	24	25	26	27	㉘	29
30	31					

☐ Sabbat   ⬤ New Moon   ◯ Full Moon

Year of the Rabbit
Herb of the Year: Ginger
International Year of Millets

March

M	T	W	T	F	S	S
		1	2	3	4	5
6	⑦	8	9	10	11	12
13	14	15	16	17	18	19
⟦20⟧	㉑	22	23	24	25	26
27	28	29	30	31		

April

M	T	W	T	F	S	S
					1	2
3	4	⑤	6	7	8	9
10	11	12	13	14	15	16
17	18	⑲	20	21	22	23
24	25	26	27	28	29	30

July

M	T	W	T	F	S	S
					1	2
③	4	5	6	7	8	9
10	11	12	13	14	15	16
⑰	18	19	20	21	22	23
24	25	26	27	28	29	30
31						

August

M	T	W	T	F	S	S
⟦1⟧	2	3	4	5	6	
7	8	9	10	11	12	13
14	15	⑯	17	18	19	20
21	22	23	24	25	26	27
28	29	30	31			

November

M	T	W	T	F	S	S
		1	2	3	4	5
6	7	8	9	10	11	12
⑬	14	15	16	17	18	19
20	21	22	23	24	25	26
㉗	28	29	30			

December

M	T	W	T	F	S	S
				1	2	3
4	5	6	7	8	9	10
11	⑫	13	14	15	16	17
18	19	20	⟦21⟧	22	23	24
25	㉖	27	28	29	30	31

∞ This year's theme is Infinite Spells

Table of Contents

Key to Symbols

Events

✸	Sabbat
⊗	Exact Astronomical Cross-Quarter
●	New Moon
◑	First Quarter
○	Full Moon
◐	Third or Last Quarter

Celestial Symbols

☿	Mercury	☽	Moon
♂	Mars	☉	Sun
♃	Jupiter	♄	Saturn
☍	Opposition	♀	Venus
☌	Conjunction		Meteor Shower
℞	Retrograde	V/C	Void of Course

Zodiac Signs

♈	Aries
♉	Taurus
♊	Gemini
♋	Cancer
♌	Leo
♍	Virgo
♎	Libra
♏	Scorpio
♐	Sagittarius
♑	Capricorn
♒	Aquarius
♓	Pisces

♣ Lucky and highly magical days.

elcome

Thank you for choosing *The Practical Witch's Almanac*! The recipes, correspondences, spells, and magical information in your almanac maintain their perennial value long after the calendar year has ended.

This year's theme is *Infinite Spells*. As you study your almanac you'll learn to use the fundamentals of magic to design spells for any occasion, and learn how to work with the natural energies of the phases of the moon, stones, herbs, colors, and more. Using your creativity and intuition, you'll be able to design spells specifically tailored to achieve your goals.

Daylight Saving Time

In March of 2022, the U.S. Senate passed legislation to make Daylight Saving Time (DST) permanent beginning in 2023. This Sunshine Protection Act will end the twice-annual changing of clocks. However, the bill must still pass the House of Representatives and then be signed by the president. This bill has not become law and is unlikely to at the time of printing, so the data in this almanac assumes the time changes will occur as normal in March and November. If it does become law, you'll subtract one hour from the times listed between March 12, 2023, and November 5, 2023. If you'd like to receive an email notification in the event that there are DST changes, sign up for the newsletter at PracticalWitch.com

Daylight Saving Time begins on March 12, 2023 at 2:00 am when you set your clock forward one hour to 3:00 am. Daylight Saving Time ends on November 5, 2023 at 2:00 am when you set your clock back one hour to 1:00 am.

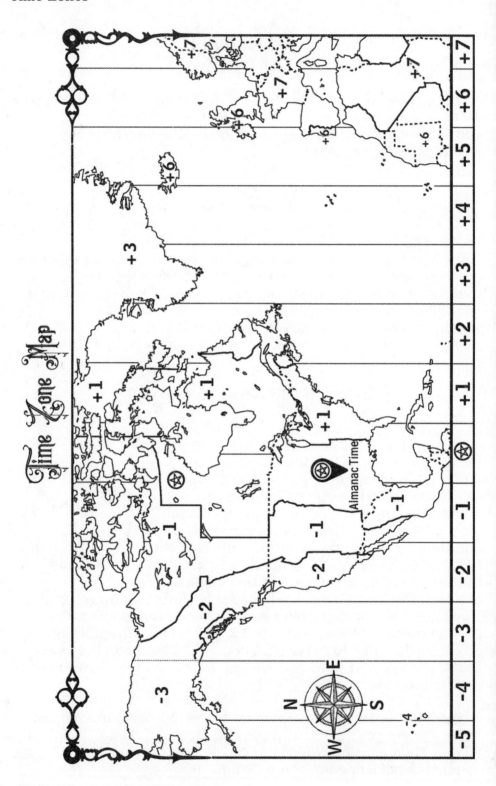

Time Zone Conversion

Your almanac is fitted to Central Time and Daylight Saving Time (DST) is accounted for when in effect. Add or subtract hours as indicated for your area.

Auckland, New Zealand +19

New Plymouth, NZ +19

Sydney, Australia +17

Melbourne, Australia +17

Cairns, Australia +16

Adelaide, Australia +16.5

Alice Springs, Australia +15.5

Tokyo, Japan +15

Perth, Australia +14

Shanghai, China +14

Hong Kong, Hong Kong +14

New Delhi, India +11.5

Moscow, Russia +9

Cairo, Egypt +8

Athens, Greece +8

Rovaniemi, Finland +8

Paris, France +7

Longyearbyen, Norway +7

Zürich, Switzerland +7

Berlin, Germany +7

Amsterdam, Netherlands +7

Madrid, Spain +7

Rome, Italy +7

Dublin, Ireland +6

Lisbon, Portugal +6

Prague, Czech Republic +6

Reykjavik, Iceland +6

Glasgow, United Kingdom +6

Ittoqqortoormiit, Greenland +5

Nuuk, Greenland +3

Halifax, Canada +2

Bridgetown, Barbados +2

Nassau, Bahamas +1

Ottawa, Canada +1

Port-au-Prince, Haiti +1

New York, NY, USA +1

Denver, CO, USA -1

Portland, OR, USA -2

Phoenix, AZ, USA -1

Honolulu, HI, USA -4

Hawaii, Puerto Rico, Guam, US Virgin Islands, and most of Arizona (except the Navajo Nation and parts of the north-east corner of the state) do not observe DST. For these or any areas without DST, subtract an hour (-1) from the time provided in your almanac from March 12 to November 5.

The Sabbats

Sabbats are seasonal festivals known for their magical energy, celestial symmetry, and spiritual significance. Each Sabbat is known by various names, reflecting differences in traditions and teachings. One coven may refer to the June solstice as *Litha*, while another will call it *Midsummer*. Regardless of the names, most witches celebrate the eight classic Sabbats of four Quarters and four Cross-Quarters.

Quarters

The four Quarter Sabbats are the two solstices and two equinoxes. These astrological events do not occur on the same day every year. These Sabbats divide the path of the sun around earth (the ecliptic) into quarters, and they fall on the ecliptic at 90° apart from each other.

Cross–Quarters

The four Cross-Quarter Sabbats are traditionally celebrated on specific days. These traditional days do not fall exactly halfway between the Quarter Sabbats.

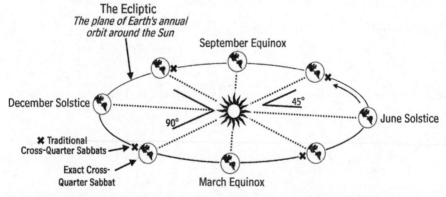

Traditional Cross-Quarter Sabbats are shown with ✖. Note that they fall just before the astronomical Cross-Quarters.

Exact Astronomical Cross-Quarters

The exact astronomical Cross-Quarter Sabbats occur when the earth is precisely halfway along the ecliptic between a solstice and an equinox. The Quarters and astronomical Cross-Quarters are 45° apart from each other.

Many witches combine the traditional Cross-Quarter Sabbat dates with the astronomical Cross-Quarters. For example, traditional Samhain celebrations begin on October 31st and continue through November 1st. The astronomical Cross-Quarter date for Samhain is November 7th, and some witches celebrate Samhain from October 31st through November 7th.

Northern & Southern Hemispheres

Which Sabbat you celebrate on a particular date depends on your tradition and location. Witches in the Southern Hemisphere (SH) may observe the same Sabbats simultaneously as those in the Northern Hemisphere (NH) if that is how they were originally trained.

However, SH witches often choose to celebrate according to the local seasons. Rather than celebrate Beltane on May 1st when it is autumn in the Southern Hemisphere, these witches may reverse the Sabbats and observe Samhain. Then on October 31st, they will be celebrating Beltane.

Remember, you are the authority in your practice! You have the final say in which Sabbats you observe, when you celebrate, and what names you use for them.

Your Traditions

Your Sabbat celebrations do not need to be elaborate. A simple activity you do on a Sabbat every year helps you attune with the rhythms of the Wheel of the Year. On Imbolc, I make candles. At the summer solstice, I harvest catnip at its peak potency. These simple tasks have been constants through the years regardless of any other rituals I observe. Try adding an activity to your Sabbats that you'll enjoy throughout your life.

Sabbat Times & Dates

Traditional Cross-Quarter Sabbats are indicated with an eight-spoked wheel ✸ as can be seen for Imbolc on February 2nd in the Northern Hemisphere and August 1st in the Southern Hemisphere.

The exact astronomical Cross-Quarter data is underneath the traditional data. For example, the Imbolc Cross-Quarter date is February 3rd at 8:27 pm Central Time. At this time, the Sun is 45° along the ecliptic between the December 2022 solstice and the March 2023 equinox.

Imbolc

This Sabbat often includes resolutions for the coming year and rituals for purification and cleansing. Physical and magical housekeeping are popular tasks. The exact Cross Quarter event ⊗ occurs a bit later than the traditional Sabbat, as noted below.

Imbolc Northern Hemisphere

✸ **Traditional Sabbat February 2**

⊗ February 3				⊗ February 4	
Pacific	Mountain	Central	Eastern	UTC	Central Europe
6:27 pm	7:27 pm	8:27 pm	9:27 pm	2.27 am	3:27 am

Imbolc Southern Hemisphere

✸ **Traditional Sabbat August 1**

⊗ August 8	
Australian Western Standard Time	New Zealand
2:21 am	6:21 am

Spring Equinox / Ostara / Vernal Equinox

Ostara is a celebration of spring, balance, new beginnings, and planting. Ostara is an excellent time to set the foundations of a project both magically and physically.

❀ Ostara Northern Hemisphere

❀ March 20					
Pacific	Mountain	Central	Eastern	UTC	Central Europe
2:24 pm	3:24 pm	4:24 pm	5:24 pm	9:24 pm	10:24 pm

❀ Ostara Southern Hemisphere

❀ September 23	
Australian Western Standard Time	New Zealand
12:50 pm	4:50 pm

Beltane

Beltane is a celebration of the power of life. Fertility, growth, joy, sensuality, and sexuality are central themes of this Sabbat. The exact Cross-Quarter event ⊗ falls precisely between the Spring Equinox and the Summer Solstice, as noted below.

Beltane Northern Hemisphere

❀ Traditional Sabbat May 1

⊗ May 5					
Pacific	Mountain	Central	Eastern	UTC	Central Europe
11:13 am	12:13 pm	1:13 pm	2:13 pm	6:13 pm	8:13 pm

Beltane Southern Hemisphere

✿ **Traditional Sabbat October 31**

⊗ November 8	
Australian Western Standard Time	New Zealand
12:18 am	*5:18 am*

Summer Solstice

Midsummer is a celebration of the sun and its power on earth. It is a great time to set out ritual tools and stones[1] to clear and neutralize their energy. The evening brings a magical time when connecting with nature spirits is said to be more accessible. This Quarter Sabbat occurs at the precise times indicated in the following tables.

✿ Summer Solstice Northern Hemisphere

June 21					
Pacific	Mountain	Central	Eastern	UTC	Central Europe
7:58 am	*8:58 am*	*9:58 am*	*10:58 am*	2:58 pm	*4:58 pm*

✿ Summer Solstice Southern Hemisphere

December 22	
Australian Western Standard Time	New Zealand
11:27 am	*4:27 pm*

Lughnasadh

Lughnasadh is a harvest celebration, and we enjoy the early fruits of our endeavors. Those projects we 'planted' in the spring are beginning to manifest. Grains and seeds are often incorporated into the festivities. The exact Cross-

---

1   Avoid leaving stones out for more than an hour as some colors may fade.

Quarter event is precisely between the Summer Solstice and the Autumnal Equinox, as noted below.

Lughnasadh Northern Hemisphere

❀ Traditional Sabbat August 1

⊗ August 7					
Pacific	Mountain	Central	Eastern	UTC	Central Europe
11:21 am	*12:21 pm*	*1:21 pm*	*2:21 pm*	6:21 pm	*8:21 pm*

Lughnasadh Southern Hemisphere

❀ Traditional Sabbat February 2

⊗ February 4	
Australian Western Standard Time	New Zealand
10:27 am	*3:27 pm*

Autumn Equinox / Mabon

This is the second harvest Sabbat and again, we see the results of the projects we 'planted' in the spring. We express gratitude and begin to reflect on the coming winter.

❀ Autumn Equinox Northern Hemisphere

September 22			September 23		
Pacific	Mountain	Central	Eastern	UTC	Central Europe
9:50 pm	*10:50 pm*	*11:50 pm*	*12:50 am*	4:50 am	*8:50 am*

❀ Autumn Equinox Southern Hemisphere

March 21	
Australian Western Standard Time	New Zealand
5:24 am	*10:24 am*

15

Samhain

Samhain is the most celebrated Sabbat and is the third and last harvest festival. We express our gratitude and reflect on life, death, and rebirth. We honor our ancestors and perform all types of magic and divination. Samhain is a highly magical time.

Samhain Northern Hemisphere

❈ Traditional Sabbat October 31

⊗ November 7					
Pacific	Mountain	Central	Eastern	UTC	Central Europe
8:18 am	9:18 am	10:18 am	11:18 am	4:18 pm	5:18 pm

Samhain Southern Hemisphere

❈ Traditional Sabbat May 1

⊗ May 6	
Australian Western Standard Time	New Zealand
2:13 am	6:13 am

Yule

This Sabbat is a celebration of the return of the sun. Feasting and gift giving are popular festivities. Most witches tend to focus on reflection on the past year and gratitude. We also consider new approaches to overcome the challenges in our lives and make plans for the coming year.

❈ Yule Northern Hemisphere

December 21				December 22	
Pacific	Mountain	Central	Eastern	UTC	Central Europe
7:27 pm	8:27 pm	9:27 pm	10:27 pm	3:27 am	4:27 am

❀ Yule Southern Hemisphere

June 21	June 22
Australian Western Standard Time	New Zealand
10:58 pm	2:58 am

The Holly King and Oak King are personifications of winter and summer in some witchcraft traditions. These plants are often displayed on altars around Yule.

Other Festivals

Hecate: Hecate (or Hekate) is honored on January 31st in some traditions, but the more popular *Night of Hecate* is November 16th. Some traditions honor Diana and Hecate from the evening of August 13th to August 16th.

Isis: Dedicants of Isis honor this Goddess on December 25th, January 6th, and March 5th.

Brigit: Brigit's day is Imbolc, from sunset on February 1st to sunset on February 2nd.

Einherjar: Some Ásatrú traditions celebrate Einherjar (the feast of the fallen) on Veterans Day, November 11th. Ancestors who have fallen in battle are honored with quiet rituals.

Moon Phases

2023 Full Moons

Jan 6, 5:07 pm (Micro Moon)[2]	Cancer ♋
Feb 5, 12:28 pm (Micro Moon)	Leo ♌
Mar 7, 6:40 am	Virgo ♍
Apr 5, 11:34 pm	Libra ♎
May 5, 12:34 pm	Scorpio ♏
Jun 3, 10:41 pm	Sagittarius ♐
Jul 3, 6:38 am (Supermoon)	Capricorn ♑
Aug 1, 1:31 pm (Supermoon)	Aquarius ♒
Aug 30, 8:35 pm (Supermoon, Blue Moon)	Pisces ♓
Sep 29, 4:57 am (Supermoon)	Aries ♈
Oct 28, 3:24 pm	Taurus ♉
Nov 27, 3:16 am	Gemini ♊
Dec 26, 6:33 pm	Cancer ♋

2023 New Moons

Jan 21, 2:53 pm (Supermoon)	Aquarius ♒
Feb 20, 1:05 am (Supermoon)	Pisces ♓
Mar 21, 12:23 pm	Aries ♈
Apr 19,11:12 pm	Aries ♈
May 19, 10:53 am (Black Moon)	Taurus ♉
Jun 17, 11:37 pm	Gemini ♊
Jul 17, 1:31 pm	Cancer ♋
Aug 16, 4:38 am (Micro Moon)	Leo ♌
Sep 14, 8:39 pm	Virgo ♍
Oct 14, 12:55 pm	Libra ♎
Nov 13, 3:27 am	Scorpio ♏
Dec 12, 5:32 pm	Sagittarius ♐

2 Supermoon, Micro Moon, Blue Moon, and Black Moon definitions can be found in the Glossary at the end of your almanac.

Eclipses

Lunar Eclipses

Lunar eclipses occur during the full moon, and the moon cycles through the waning, new, and waxing phases during an eclipse. The unification of earth and moon energies can be felt as the earth's shadow falls over the moon.

You might find this an excellent time to focus on the Goddess, work on your psychic skills, perform divination, or charge a special eclipse moon water. Advanced spells with multiple phases work well during lunar eclipses. As the eclipse begins, focus on banishing, cleansing, or ridding yourself of harmful behaviors. As the eclipse ends, focus on attraction, drawing, peace, forming new positive behaviors, or abundance.

May 5 Penumbral Lunar Eclipse

A penumbral eclipse occurs when the earth's diffuse outer shadow falls on the moon's surface. *Pen* is from the Latin *pœne* meaning "nearly" or "almost." See it in South and East Europe, Australia, Africa, and most of Asia.

	UTC	Central Time
Eclipse Begins	15:14	10:14 am
Peak Eclipse	17:22	12:22 pm
Eclipse Ends	19:31	2:31 pm

Oct 28 Partial Lunar Eclipse

A partial lunar eclipse occurs when earth's *umbra* (Latin for shadow) appears to take a bite out of the moon. You can see this one in Europe, Asia, Australia, Africa, and the farthest eastern parts of North and South America.

	UTC	Central Time
Eclipse Begins	18:01	1:01 pm
Peak Eclipse	20:14	3:14 pm
Eclipse Ends	22:26	5:26 pm

Solar Eclipses

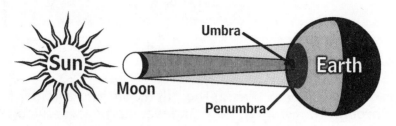

You can work some interesting magic during a solar eclipse. Because a solar eclipse can only occur during the new moon, you'll be working with new moon energy and the power of the sun. At the beginning of a solar eclipse, you could focus on ridding yourself of bane. As the eclipse passes, focus on growth and attraction.

April 19-20 Total Solar Eclipse

The moon will completely obscure the sun leaving just the sun's corona visible. See it in South and East Asia, Indonesia, Australia, and Antarctica.

	UTC	Central Time
Eclipse Begins	Apr 20, 01:34	Apr 19, 8:34 pm
Peak Eclipse	Apr 20, 04:16	Apr 19, 11:16 pm
Eclipse Ends	Apr 20, 06:59	Apr 20, 1:59 am

Oct 14 Annular Solar Eclipse

The moon is near apogee for this eclipse. Because the moon is far away, it appears smaller and will not cover the entire sun. This will leave a thin ring of the sun uncovered for what is called an annular solar eclipse. This is the only eclipse in 2023 that is easily visible in much of the Western U.S. and Central America. You can also see it in South America, Columbia, and Brazil.

	UTC	Central Time
Eclipse Begins	15:03	10:03 am
Peak Eclipse	17:59	12:59 pm
Eclipse ends	20:55	3:55 pm

Apogee & Perigee

Apogee (ăp′ə-jē) is the point in the moon's orbit when it is farthest away from earth. Perigee (pĕr′ə-jē) is the point in its orbit when it is closest to earth.

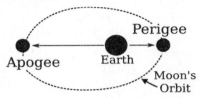

You may find it enlightening to note the times of apogee and perigee in your book of shadows, divination journal, spell records, or when you are tracking your cycles. When working with lunar energies, consider both the phase of the moon and its distance from the earth.

Just as the moon causes the tides and winds, it has a powerful affect on us. By keeping careful records, you'll be able to identify patterns of how the distance of the moon affects you. The moon can be nearly 31,000 miles closer to us at perigee.

Perigee	Apogee
Jan 21, 2:56 pm[3]	Jan 8, 3:19 am
Feb 19, 3:05 am	Feb 4, 2:54 am
Mar 19, 10:12 am	Mar 3, 12:00 pm
Apr 15, 9:23 pm	Mar 31, 6:16 am
May 11, 12:05 am	Apr 28, 1:43 am
Jun 6. 6:06 pm	May 25, 8:39 pm
Jul 4. 5:24 pm	Jun 22, 1:30 pm
Aug 2. 12:52 am	Jul 20, 1:56 am
Aug 30. 10:54 am	**Aug 16, 6:54 am[4]**
Sep 27, 7:59 pm	Sep 12, 10:42 am
Oct 25, 10:02 pm	Oct 9, 10:41 pm
Nov 21, 3:01 pm	Nov 6, 3:48 pm
Dec 16, 12:52 pm	Dec 4, 12:41 pm

---

3   January 21, 2:53 pm is the new moon. A few minutes later it makes its closest approach to earth for the entire year. This is a super new moon.
4   August 16, 4:38 am is the new moon. A couple of hours later the moon is the farthest from earth for the entire year. This is a micro new moon.

Major Holidays & Observances

This almanac emphasizes earth-based spiritual traditions, but we don't live in a bubble. The table on the next page covers all major events celebrated by a large majority of people. Common holidays are listed in your Planner Pages, but the observances of the Abrahamic religions are not. With over 20% of Americans celebrating Easter, millions of Hindus celebrating Holi, and over 1.6 billion people celebrating Ramadan, there is a good chance that your friends, coworkers, or neighbors are celebrating some of the major holidays and observances.

It is good to be aware of the U.S. federal holidays due to their significance to U.S. citizens. It is also important to note the federal holidays because banks, government buildings, post offices, many schools, and other public facilities are closed. When a federal holiday falls on a Saturday, the preceding Friday is treated as the holiday for closures, pay, and leave purposes. When a holiday falls on a Sunday, the following Monday is treated as the holiday. Two federal holidays fall on the weekend this year. New Year's Day is on Sunday, January 1st, so it is observed on Monday, January 2nd. Veterans Day is on Saturday, November 11th, and is observed on Friday, November 10th.

Notes

- August 26th is Women's Equality Day. This holiday commemorates the 1920 certification of the 19th Amendment to the Constitution, granting women the right to vote. What began in Seneca Falls, NY in 1848 became a massive (and peaceful) civil rights movement by women.
- Feb. 20th is known as "Presidents' Day" but it is officially "Washington's Birthday" in U.S. code Title 5, § 6103. October 9th is officially "Columbus Day" but I've used the more appropriate "Indigenous People's Day."

Abbreviations

- **U.S. Federal Holidays are in bold.**
- (C) Christian, (O) Orthodox Christian, (H) Hindu, (M) Muslim, (J) Jewish.
- Events without notations such as Mother's Day and Cyber Monday are general observances and are not specifically religious or official.

Major Holidays & Observances

Jan 1, New Year's Day	May 26, Shavuot (J)
Jan 2, New Year's Day Observed	May 28, Pentecost (C)
Jan 6, Epiphany (C)	**May 29, Memorial Day**
Jan 7, Christmas Day (O)	Jun 8, Corpus Christi (C)
Jan 14, New Year (O)	Jun 18, Fathers' Day
Jan 14, Makar Sankranti (H)	Jun 19, Rath Yatra (H)
Jan 16, Martin Luther King Day	**Jun 19, Juneteenth**
Jan 22, Chinese New Year	Jun 28, Day of Arafat (M)
Feb 2, Groundhog Day	Jun 29, Eid al-Adha (M)
Feb 6, Tu B'Shevat (J)	**Jul 4, Independence Day**
Feb 14, Valentine's Day	Jul 19, Muharram (M)
Feb 18, Maha Shivaratri (H)	Jul 27, Tisha B'Av (J)
Feb 18, Isra and Mi'raj (M)	Jul 28, Ashura (M)
Feb 20, Presidents' Day	Aug 15, Assumption of Mary (C)
Feb 21, Mardi Gras (C)	Aug 21, Senior Citizens Day
Feb 22, Ash Wednesday (C)	Aug 26, Women's Equality Day
Feb 22, Lent (C)	Aug 30, Raksha Bandhan (H)
Mar 2, Read Across America Day	**Sep 4, Labor Day**
Mar 3, Employee Appreciation Day	Sep 6, Krishna Janmashtami (H)
Mar 7, Purim (J)	Sep 10, Grandparents Day
Mar 8, Laylat al Bara'at (M)	Sept 16, Rosh Hashanah (J)
Mar 8, Holi (H)	Sep 18, Ganesh Chaturthi (H)
Mar 17, St. Patrick's Day	Sept 25, Yom Kippur (J)
Mar 22 to Apr 21, Ramadan (M)	Sep 27, The Prophet's Birthday (M)
Mar 30, Rama Navami (H)	Sep 30, Sukkot (J)
Apr 1, April Fools' Day	Oct 7, Shemini Atzeret (J)
Apr 2, Palm Sunday (C)	Oct 8, Simchat Torah (J)
Apr 6 to Apr 13 Passover (J)	Oct 9, Leif Erikson Day
Apr 6, Maundy Thursday (C)	**Oct 9, Indigenous People's Day**
Apr 7, Good Friday (C)	Oct 15, Navratri (H)
Apr 8, Holy Saturday (C)	Oct 23, Dussehra (H)
Apr 9, Easter (C)	Oct 31, Halloween
Apr 10, Easter Monday (C)	Nov 1, All Saints' Day (C)
Apr 11, Library Workers Day	Nov 2, All Souls Day (C)
Apr 13, Thomas Jefferson Birthday	**Nov 10, Veterans Day Observed**
Apr 14, Good Friday (O)	Nov 11, Veterans Day
Apr 15, Tax Day	Nov 12, Diwali (H)
Apr 16, Easter (O)	**Nov 23, Thanksgiving Day**
Apr 17, Yom Hashoah (J)	Nov 24, Black Friday
Apr 18, Laylat al Qadr (M)	Nov 27, Cyber Monday
Apr 22, Earth Day	Dec 3, Advent (C)
Apr 22, Eid al-Fitr (M)	Dec 6, St Nicholas Day (C)
Apr 28, Arbor Day	Dec 7, Pearl Harbor Remembrance
May 1, May Day	Dec 8 to 15, Hanukkah (J)
May 4, National Day of Prayer	Dec 17, Wright Brothers Day
May 5, Cinco de Mayo	Dec 24, Christmas Eve (C)
May 6, National Nurses Day	**Dec 25, Christmas Day**
May 9, Lag BaOmer (J)	Dec 26 to Jan 1, Kwanzaa
May 14, Mother's Day	Dec 31, New Year's Eve

December – January

December 2022						
Mo	Tu	We	Th	Fr	Sa	Su
			1	2	3	4
5	6	7	8	9	10	11
12	13	14	15	16	17	18
19	20	21	22	23	24	25
26	27	28	29	30	31	

January 2023						
Mo	Tu	We	Th	Fr	Sa	Su
						1
2	3	4	5	6	7	8
9	10	11	12	13	14	15
16	17	18	19	20	21	22
23	24	25	26	27	28	29
30	31					

Monday 26

Tuesday 27

Wednesday 28

National Card Playing Day

Thursday 29

☿℞ Begins

Friday 30

Saturday 31

New Year's Eve

Sunday, January 1

New Year's Day

Jan 2 – 8

January 2023						
Mo	Tu	We	Th	Fr	Sa	Su
						1
2	3	4	5	6	7	8
9	10	11	12	13	14	15
16	17	18	19	20	21	22
23	24	25	26	27	28	29
30	31					

Monday 2

☽ VoC 4:16 pm
☽ ♊ 8:44 pm
New Year's Day Observed (U.S. Federal Holiday)

Tuesday 3

Festival of Sleep Day
☄ Quadrantid Meteor Shower

Wednesday 4

Trivia Day
☽V/C 6:07 pm
☉ Perihelion 10:17 am
☄ Quadrantid Meteor Shower

Thursday 5

☽♋ 8:15 am
Whip Cream Day

Friday 6

Bean Day
Befana Day
○ 5:07 pm Micro Full Moon

Saturday 7

☽V/C 4:22 pm
☽♌ 8:40 pm
Programmers' Day
Galileo discovers four of Jupiter's moons in 1610

Sunday 8

Bubble Bath Day

January 9–15

| | | January 2023 | | | | |
Mo	Tu	We	Th	Fr	Sa	Su
						1
2	3	4	5	6	7	8
9	10	11	12	13	14	15
16	17	18	19	20	21	22
23	24	25	26	27	28	29
30	31					

Monday 9

7:52 pm ☽V/C
Coming of Age Day (Japan)

Tuesday 10

☽♍ 9:16 am
Peculiar People Day

Wednesday 11

Thursday 12

☽V/C 5:06 pm
☽♎ 8:57 pm
Hot Tea Day

Friday 13

Saturday 14

Sunday 15

☽V/C 2:39 am
☽♏ 6:09 am
National Hat Day

January 16–22

January 2023

Mo	Tu	We	Th	Fr	Sa	Su
						1
2	3	4	5	6	7	8
9	10	11	12	13	14	15
16	17	18	19	20	21	22
23	24	25	26	27	28	29
30	31					

Monday 16

Appreciate a Dragon Day
Martin Luther King Day (U.S. Federal Holiday)

Tuesday 17

☽V/C 8:26 am
☽♐ 11:33 am

Wednesday 18

☿℞ Ends

Thursday 19

☽V/C 4:08 am
☽♑ 1:12 pm

Friday 20

☉♒ 2:30 am Sun enters Aquarius

Saturday 21

♣
☽V/C 9:51 am
☽♒ 12:29 pm
National Granola Bar Day
● Super New Moon 2:53 pm

Sunday 22

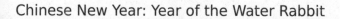

Chinese New Year: Year of the Water Rabbit

January 23–29

	January 2023					
Mo	Tu	We	Th	Fr	Sa	Su
						1
2	3	4	5	6	7	8
9	10	11	12	13	14	15
16	17	18	19	20	21	22
23	24	25	26	27	28	29
30	31					

Monday 23

☽V/C 4:18 am
☽⋇ 11:36 am

Tuesday 24

Compliment Day

Wednesday 25

Opposite Day
☽V/C 10:11 am
☽♈ 12:48 pm

Thursday 26

Australia Day

Friday 27

☽V/C 3:00 pm
☽♉ 5:43 pm
Chocolate Cake Day

Saturday 28

National Seed Swap Day

Sunday 29

☽V/C 11:51 pm

January 30–February 5

January 2023						
Mo	Tu	We	Th	Fr	Sa	Su
						1
2	3	4	5	6	7	8
9	10	11	12	13	14	15
16	17	18	19	20	21	22
23	24	25	26	27	28	29
30	31					

February 2023						
Mo	Tu	We	Th	Fr	Sa	Su
		1	2	3	4	5
6	7	8	9	10	11	12
13	14	15	16	17	18	19
20	21	22	23	24	25	26
27	28					

Monday 30

☽Ⅱ 2:35 am
☿ Mercury at Greatest Western Elongation,
   view the planet low in the eastern sky just before sunrise

Tuesday 31

National Hot Chocolate Day

Wednesday 1

☽V/C 5:57 am
☽♋ 2:12 pm
National Freedom Day

Thursday 2

Groundhog Day
❇ Sabbat Imbolc/Lughnasadh

Friday 3

⊗ Exact Cross-Quarter 8:27 pm: Imbolc/Lughnasadh

Saturday 4

☽V/C 12:18 am
☽♌ 2:49 am
Rosa Parks Day

Sunday 5

Lantern Festival
○ Micro Full Moon 12:28 pm

February 6–12

Mo	Tu	We	Th	Fr	Sa	Su
		1	2	3	4	5
6	7	8	9	10	11	12
13	14	15	16	17	18	19
20	21	22	23	24	25	26
27	28					

February 2023

Monday 6

☽V/C 8:15 am
☽♍ 3:14 pm
Waitangi Day (New Zealand)

Tuesday 7

Wednesday 8

National Kite Flying Day

Thursday 9

☽V/C 12:39 am
☽♎ 2:47 am
National Pizza Day

Friday 10

Saturday 11

☽♎ 2:47 am
☽♏ 12:35 pm
National Foundation Day (Japan)

Sunday 12

February 13–19

February 2023						
Mo	Tu	We	Th	Fr	Sa	Su
		1	2	3	4	5
6	7	8	9	10	11	12
13	14	15	16	17	18	19
20	21	22	23	24	25	26
27	28					

Monday 13

☽V/C 5:51 pm
☽♐ 7:31 pm

Tuesday 14

Valentine's Day

Wednesday 15

☽V/C 7:05 pm
☽♑ 11:00 pm
Susan B. Anthony Day

Thursday 16

ħ☌☉ Saturn in conjunction with Sun 10:38 am

Friday 17

☽V/C 10:17 pm
☽≈ 11:35 pm
Carnival (Brazil)

Saturday 18

☉⁂ 4:35 pm Sun enters Pisces

Sunday 19

☽V/C 8:00 pm
☽⁂ 10:56 pm

February 20–26

Mo	Tu	We	Th	Fr	Sa	Su
		1	2	3	4	5
6	7	8	9	10	11	12
13	14	15	16	17	18	19
20	21	22	23	24	25	26
27	28					

February 2023

Monday 20

♣
World Day of Social Justice
● Super New Moon 1:05 am
Presidents' Day (U.S. Federal Holiday)

Tuesday 21

Mardi Gras
☽V/C 10:05 pm
☽♈ 11:14 pm
Barbara Jordan's Birthday

Wednesday 22

Sybil Leek's Birthday

Thursday 23

National Chili Day
Emperors Birthday (Japan)
National Dog Biscuit Day

Friday 24

☽V/C 1:21 am
☽♉ 2:29 am

Saturday 25

Sunday 26

☽V/C 8:42 am
☽♊ 9:48 am

February 27–March 5

February 2023						
Mo	Tu	We	Th	Fr	Sa	Su
		1	2	3	4	5
6	7	8	9	10	11	12
13	14	15	16	17	18	19
20	21	22	23	24	25	26
27	28					

March 2023						
Mo	Tu	We	Th	Fr	Sa	Su
		1	2	3	4	5
6	7	8	9	10	11	12
13	14	15	16	17	18	19
20	21	22	23	24	25	26
27	28	29	30	31		

Monday 27

National Retro Day

Tuesday 28

)V/C 7:06 pm
) ♋ 8:40 pm

Wednesday 1

Zero Discrimination Day

Thursday 2

Read Across America Day

Friday 3

☽V/C 8:22 am
☽♌ 9:16 am
World Wildlife Day
Employee Appreciation Day

Saturday 4

Sunday 5

☽V/C 9:18 pm
☽♍ 9:39 pm

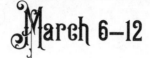 **March 6–12**

| | | March 2023 | | | | |
Mo	Tu	We	Th	Fr	Sa	Su
		1	2	3	4	5
6	7	8	9	10	11	12
13	14	15	16	17	18	19
20	21	22	23	24	25	26
27	28	29	30	31		

Monday 6

Tuesday 7

National Cereal Day
○ Full Moon 6:40 am

Wednesday 8

☽V/C 8:07 am
☽♎ 8:44 am
International Women's Day

Thursday 9

Friday 10

☾V/C 5:36 pm
☾♏ 6:06 pm
Harriet Tubman's Birthday

Saturday 11

Douglas Adams's Birthday

Sunday 12

National Plant a Flower Day
Daylight Saving Time Begins

March 13–19

Mo	Tu	We	Th	Fr	Sa	Su
		1	2	3	4	5
6	7	8	9	10	11	12
13	14	15	16	17	18	19
20	21	22	23	24	25	26
27	28	29	30	31		

March 2023

Monday 13

☽V/C 1:58 am
☽♐ 2:21 am

Tuesday 14

Pi Day
Genius Day
Albert Einsteins's Birthday

Wednesday 15

☽V/C 3:49 am
☽♑ 7:06 am

Thursday 16

Friday 17

☽V/C 9:13 am
☽≈ 9:25 am

Saturday 18

National Awkward Moments Day

Sunday 19

☽V/C 5:32 am
☽♓ 10:12 am

March 20–26

Mo	Tu	We	Th	Fr	Sa	Su
		1	2	3	4	5
6	7	8	9	10	11	12
13	14	15	16	17	18	19
20	21	22	23	24	25	26
27	28	29	30	31		

March 2023

Monday 20

☉♈ 4:24 pm Sun enters Aries
International Day of Happiness
❀ Sabbat 4:24 pm: Spring Equinox/Autumn Equinox

Tuesday 21

☽V/C 10:57 am
☽♈ 11:02 am
● New Moon 12:23 pm
International Day of Forests | World Poetry Day
World Day to Eliminate Racial Discrimination

Wednesday 22

World Water Day

Thursday 23

☽V/C 12:12 pm
☽♉ 1:42 pm
Puppy Day

Friday 24

National Chocolate Covered Raisin Day

Saturday 25

☽V/C 11:18 am
☽♊ 7:42 pm

Sunday 26

Wear a Hat Day

March 27–April 2

March 2023

Mo	Tu	We	Th	Fr	Sa	Su
		1	2	3	4	5
6	7	8	9	10	11	12
13	14	15	16	17	18	19
20	21	22	23	24	25	26
27	28	29	30	31		

April 2023

Mo	Tu	We	Th	Fr	Sa	Su
					1	2
3	4	5	6	7	8	9
10	11	12	13	14	15	16
17	18	19	20	21	22	23
24	25	26	27	28	29	30

Monday 27

☽V/C 8:39 pm

Tuesday 28

☽♋ 5:22 am
Weed Appreciation Day

Wednesday 29

Thursday 30

☽V/C 8:45 am
☽♌ 5:31 pm

Friday 31

Saturday 1

April Fools' Day

Sunday 2

☽V/C 1:02 am
☽♍ 5:58 am

April 3–9

April 2023						
Mo	Tu	We	Th	Fr	Sa	Su
					1	2
3	4	5	6	7	8	9
10	11	12	13	14	15	16
17	18	19	20	21	22	23
24	25	26	27	28	29	30

Monday 3

National Find a Rainbow Day

Tuesday 4

☽V/C 8:49 am
☽♎ 4:51 pm
Maya Angelou's Birthday 2023

Wednesday 5

○ Full Moon 11:34 pm

Thursday 6

☽V/C 7:42 am
National Tartan Day

Friday 7

☽♏ 1:30 am
United Nations World Health Day

Saturday 8

International Romani Day

Sunday 9

☽V/C 4:08 am
☽♐ 7:57 am
National Name Yourself Day

April 10–16

April 2023

Mo	Tu	We	Th	Fr	Sa	Su
					1	2
3	4	5	6	7	8	9
10	11	12	13	14	15	16
17	18	19	20	21	22	23
24	25	26	27	28	29	30

Monday 10

Tuesday 11

☽V/C 5:47 am
☽♑ 12:33 pm
National Pet Day
♃ ☌ ☉ 4:55 pm Jupiter in Conjunction with Sun
☿ Mercury at Greatest Eastern Elongation,
  view the planet low in the western sky just after sunset.

Wednesday 12

International Day of Human Space Flight

Thursday 13

Scrabble Day
☽V/C 9:13 am
☽≈ 3:42 pm

Friday 14

National Library Workers Day

Saturday 15

☽V/C 10:15 am
☽⊬ 5:57 pm

Sunday 16

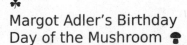

♣
Margot Adler's Birthday
Day of the Mushroom

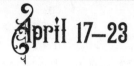
April 17–23

Mo	Tu	We	Th	Fr	Sa	Su
					1	2
3	4	5	6	7	8	9
10	11	12	13	14	15	16
17	18	19	20	21	22	23
24	25	26	27	28	29	30

April 2023

Monday 17

☽V/C 1:56 pm
☽♈ 8:10 pm
National Haiku Poetry Day

Tuesday 18

U.S. Tax Day

Wednesday 19

Bicycle Day
☽V/C 11:12 pm
☽♉ 11:30 pm
☉ Total Solar Eclipse 11:16 pm
● New Moon 11:12 pm

Thursday 20

🌿420
☉♉ 3:14 am Sun enters Taurus

Friday 21

☿℞ Begins
☽V/C 10:40 pm

Saturday 22

Earth Day
☽♊ 5:11 am
National Jelly Bean Day
☄ Lyrid Meteor Shower

Sunday 23

☄ Lyrid Meteor Shower
Order of the Garter Established

April 24–30

Mo	Tu	We	Th	Fr	Sa	Su
					1	2
3	4	5	6	7	8	9
10	11	12	13	14	15	16
17	18	19	20	21	22	23
24	25	26	27	28	29	30

April 2023

Monday 24

☽V/C 7:14 am
☽♋ 1:59 pm

Tuesday 25

ANZAC Day
National Telephone Day

Wednesday 26

☽V/C 6:40 pm
National Pretzel Day
Administrative Professionals Day

Thursday 27

☽♌ 1:30 am
National Tell a Story Day

Friday 28

Arbor Day
National Superhero Day

Saturday 29

Shōwa Day
☽V/C 5:52 am
☽♍ 1:59 pm
National Zipper Day

Sunday 30

International Jazz Day

May 1–7

Mo	Tu	We	Th	Fr	Sa	Su
May 2023						
1	2	3	4	5	6	7
8	9	10	11	12	13	14
15	16	17	18	19	20	21
22	23	24	25	26	27	28
29	30	31				

Monday 1

Lei Day
☽V/C 6:52 pm
WitchAcademy.org Founded 1996
❀ Sabbat: Beltane/Samhain

Tuesday 2

☽♎ 1:09 am

Wednesday 3

World Press Freedom Day

Thursday 4

)V/C 4:16 am
)♏ 9:33 am
Greenery Day (Japan)
Star Wars Day, *May the Fourth be with You*

Friday 5

Cinco de Mayo
Childrens Day (Japan)
○ Full Moon 12:34 pm
⁘ Eta-Aquarid Meteor Shower
Penumbral Lunar Eclipse 12:22 pm
⊗ Exact Cross-Quarter 1:13 pm: Beltane/Samhain

Saturday 6

)V/C 9:37 am
)♐ 3:04 pm
Herb Day
National Nurses Day
⁘ Eta-Aquarid Meteor Shower

Sunday 7

⁘ Eta-Aquarid Meteor Shower

May 8–14

May 2023

Mo	Tu	We	Th	Fr	Sa	Su
1	2	3	4	5	6	7
8	9	10	11	12	13	14
15	16	17	18	19	20	21
22	23	24	25	26	27	28
29	30	31				

Monday 8

☽V/C 3:27 pm
☽♑ 6:33 pm

Tuesday 9

Wednesday 10

☽V/C 6:52 pm
☽♒ 9:06 pm
Christopher Penczak's Birthday

Thursday 11

♣

Friday 12

☽V/C 10:15 pm
☽⚹ 11:39 pm
International Nurses Day

Saturday 13

World Migratory Bird Day

Sunday 14

☽V/C 9:56 pm
☿℞ Ends
Mother's Day

May 15–21

May 2023

Mo	Tu	We	Th	Fr	Sa	Su
1	2	3	4	5	6	7
8	9	10	11	12	13	14
15	16	17	18	19	20	21
22	23	24	25	26	27	28
29	30	31				

Monday 15

☽♈ 2:56 am

Tuesday 16

Honor Our LGBT Elders Day

Wednesday 17

☽V/C 4:09 am
☽♉ 7:28 am

Thursday 18

Friday 19

☽V/C 12:50 pm
☽♊ 1:48 pm
Malcolm X's Birthday
● New Moon 10:53 am (Black Moon)

Saturday 20

Sunday 21

☽V/C 5:11 pm
☽♋ 10:29 pm
☉♊ 2:10 am Sun enters Gemini
Cultural Diversity Day
Gwydion Pendderwen's Birthday

May 22–28

Mo	Tu	We	Th	Fr	Sa	Su
1	2	3	4	5	6	7
8	9	10	11	12	13	14
15	16	17	18	19	20	21
22	23	24	25	26	27	28
29	30	31				

May 2023

Monday 22

Victoria Day

Tuesday 23

National Lucky Penny Day

Wednesday 24

☽V/C 4:11 am
☽♌ 9:35 am
National Scavenger Hunt Day

Thursday 25

Towel Day

Friday 26

☽V/C 1:38 am
☽♍ 10:05 pm

Saturday 27

Morning Glory Zell-Ravenheart's Birthday

Sunday 28

May 29–June 4

Mo	Tu	We	Th	Fr	Sa	Su
\multicolumn{7}{c}{May 2023}

May 2023

Mo	Tu	We	Th	Fr	Sa	Su
1	2	3	4	5	6	7
8	9	10	11	12	13	14
15	16	17	18	19	20	21
22	23	24	25	26	27	28
29	30	31				

June 2023

Mo	Tu	We	Th	Fr	Sa	Su
			1	2	3	4
5	6	7	8	9	10	11
12	13	14	15	16	17	18
19	20	21	22	23	24	25
26	27	28	29	30		

Monday 29

☽V/C 4:45 am
☽♎ 9:51 am
Memorial Day (U.S. Federal Holiday)
☿ Mercury at Greatest Western Elongation
  view the planet low in the eastern sky just before sunrise.

Tuesday 30

Wednesday 31

☽V/C 9:53 am
☽♏ 6:45 pm

Thursday 1

National Go Barefoot Day

Friday 2

☽V/C 7:50 pm

Saturday 3

☽♐ 12:04 am
National Repeat Day
○ Full Moon 10:41 pm
Marion Zimmer Bradley's Birthday

Sunday 4

☽V/C 10:23 pm
♀ Venus at Greatest Eastern Elongation,
    view the planet in the western sky after sunset.

June 5–11

			June 2023			
Mo	Tu	We	Th	Fr	Sa	Su
			1	2	3	4
5	6	7	8	9	10	11
12	13	14	15	16	17	18
19	20	21	22	23	24	25
26	27	28	29	30		

Monday 5

☽♑ 2:31 am
World Environment Day

Tuesday 6

♣
☽V/C 11:39 pm

Wednesday 7

☽≈ 3:42 am

Thursday 8

☽V/C 11:23 pm
World Oceans Day
National Best Friend Day

Friday 9

☽⚹ 5:14 am
National Strawberry Rhubarb Pie Day

Saturday 10

National Iced Tea Day

Sunday 11

☽V/C 8:19 am
☽♈ 8:21 am

June 12–18

Monday 12

Tuesday 13

☽V/C 1:26 pm
Gerald Gardner's Birthday

Wednesday 14

Thursday 15

☽V/C 8:36 pm
☽♊ 8:46 pm
Nature Photography Day

Friday 16

National Fudge Day

Saturday 17

Starhawk's Birthday
● New Moon 11:37 pm

Sunday 18

Father's Day
☽V/C 1:23 am
☽♋ 5:58 am
National Go Fishing Day

June 19-25

Mo	Tu	We	Th	Fr	Sa	Su
			1	2	3	4
5	6	7	8	9	10	11
12	13	14	15	16	17	18
19	20	21	22	23	24	25
26	27	28	29	30		

June 2023

Monday 19

Juneteenth (U.S. Federal Holiday)

Tuesday 20

☽V/C 4:43 pm
☽♌ 5:04 pm
American Eagle Day
World Refugee Day

Wednesday 21

International Day of Yoga
☉♋ 9:58 am Sun enters Cancer
✿ Sabbat 9:58 am: Summer Solstice/Winter Solstice

Thursday 22

☽V/C 12:00 pm

Friday 23

☽♍ 5:35 am

Saturday 24

Janet Farrar's Birthday
Take Your Dog to Work Day

Sunday 25

☽V/C 5:24 pm
☽♎ 5:57 pm
Day of the Seafarer

June 26–July 2

	June 2023					
Mo	Tu	We	Th	Fr	Sa	Su
			1	2	3	4
5	6	7	8	9	10	11
12	13	14	15	16	17	18
19	20	21	22	23	24	25
26	27	28	29	30		

	July 2023					
Mo	Tu	We	Th	Fr	Sa	Su
					1	2
3	4	5	6	7	8	9
10	11	12	13	14	15	16
17	18	19	20	21	22	23
24	25	26	27	28	29	30
31						

Monday 26

National Canoe Day

Tuesday 27

Scott Cunningham's Birthday

Wednesday 28

☽V/C 3:18 am
☽♏ 3:56 am
Stewart Farrar's Birthday

Thursday 29

National Camera Day

Friday 30

☽V/C 9:20 am
☽♐ 10:00 am
International Asteroid Day

Saturday 1

International Joke Day
☿☌☉ Mercury at Superior Solar Conjunction 12:12 am

Sunday 2

☽V/C 8:33 am
☽♑ 12:20 pm
 World UFO Day

July 3–9

Mo	Tu	We	Th	Fr	Sa	Su
					1	2
3	4	5	6	7	8	9
10	11	12	13	14	15	16
17	18	19	20	21	22	23
24	25	26	27	28	29	30
31						

July 2023

Monday 3

♣
Compliment Your Mirror Day
○ Full Moon 6:38 am (Supermoon)

Tuesday 4

☽V/C 11:45 am
☽≈ 12:30 pm
Independence Day (U.S. Federal Holiday)

Wednesday 5

Thursday 6

☽V/C 8:41 am
☽⚹ 12:33 pm
International Kissing Day
⊙ Aphelion 3:06 pm (Earth farthest from Sun for the year)

Friday 7

World Chocolate Day
Global Forgiveness Day

Saturday 8

☽V/C 1:21 pm
☽♈ 2:19 pm

Sunday 9

July 10–16

July 2023

Mo	Tu	We	Th	Fr	Sa	Su
					1	2
3	4	5	6	7	8	9
10	11	12	13	14	15	16
17	18	19	20	21	22	23
24	25	26	27	28	29	30
31						

Monday 10

☽V/C 6:10 pm
☽♉ 6:56 pm

Tuesday 11

World Population Day

Wednesday 12

Thursday 13

☽V/C 1:10 am
☽♊ 2:26 am
Margaret Murray's Birthday

Friday 14

Saturday 15

☽V/C 7:35 am
☽♋ 12:14 pm
National Give Something Away Day

Sunday 16

July 17–23

July 2023

Mo	Tu	We	Th	Fr	Sa	Su
					1	2
3	4	5	6	7	8	9
10	11	12	13	14	15	16
17	18	19	20	21	22	23
24	25	26	27	28	29	30
31						

Monday 17

☽V/C 10:05 pm
☽♌ 11:40 pm
☺ World Emoji Day
● New Moon 1:31 pm
Paul Stamets's Birthday

Tuesday 18

Mandela Day

Wednesday 19

Thursday 20

☽V/C 9:08 am
☽♍ 12:13 pm
Moon Landing Day 2023

Friday 21

Saturday 22

☽V/C 11:05 pm
☉♌ 8:51pm Sun enters Leo

Sunday 23

Parents' Day
☽♎ 12:54 am

July 24–30

| | | July 2023 | | | | |
Mo	Tu	We	Th	Fr	Sa	Su
					1	2
3	4	5	6	7	8	9
10	11	12	13	14	15	16
17	18	19	20	21	22	23
24	25	26	27	28	29	30
31						

Monday 24

National Drive-Thru Day

Tuesday 25

☽V/C 10:05 am
☽♏ 11:56 am

Wednesday 26

National Bagelfest Day

Thursday 27

☽V/C 5:35 pm
☽♐ 7:24 pm

Friday 28

⁂ Delta-Aquarid Meteor Shower

Saturday 29

☽V/C 6:51 pm
☽♑ 10:44 pm
⁂ Delta-Aquarid Meteor Shower

Sunday 30

National Cheesecake Day
International Day of Friendship

July 31–August 6

July 2023

Mo	Tu	We	Th	Fr	Sa	Su
					1	2
3	4	5	6	7	8	9
10	11	12	13	14	15	16
17	18	19	20	21	22	23
24	25	26	27	28	29	30
31						

August 2023

Mo	Tu	We	Th	Fr	Sa	Su
	1	2	3	4	5	6
7	8	9	10	11	12	13
14	15	16	17	18	19	20
21	22	23	24	25	26	27
28	29	30	31			

Monday 31

☽V/C 9:12 pm
☽≈ 10:58 pm

Tuesday 1

♣
Jerry Garcia's Birthday
❈ Sabbat: Lughnasadh/Imbolc
○ Full Moon 1:31 pm (Supermoon)

Wednesday 2

♣
☽V/C 4:15 pm
☽✶ 10:06 pm
National Coloring Book Day

Thursday 3

Grab Some Nuts Day

Friday 4

☽V/C 8:20 pm
☽♈ 10:20 pm

Saturday 5

Today the Mars Curiosity Rover celebrates its anniversary
by singing the Happy Birthday Song to itself on Mars.

Sunday 6

☽V/C 11:12 pm

August 7–13

Mo	Tu	We	Th	Fr	Sa	Su
	1	2	3	4	5	6
7	8	9	10	11	12	13
14	15	16	17	18	19	20
21	22	23	24	25	26	27
28	29	30	31			

August 2023

Monday 7

)ʘ 1:25 am
⊗ Exact Cross-Quarter 1:21 pm: Lughnasadh/Imbolc

Tuesday 8

Wednesday 9

)V/C 5:38 am
)Ⅱ 8:05 am
National Book Lovers Day

Thursday 10

Lazy Day
 National S'mores Day
☿ Mercury at Greatest Eastern Elongation
  view the planet low in the western sky after sunset.

Friday 11

☽V/C 12:27 pm
☽♋ 5:52 pm

Saturday 12

 Perseid Meteor Shower

Sunday 13

 Perseid Meteor Shower
International Lefthanders Day

August 14–20

Mo	Tu	We	Th	Fr	Sa	Su
	1	2	3	4	5	6
7	8	9	10	11	12	13
14	15	16	17	18	19	20
21	22	23	24	25	26	27
28	29	30	31			

August 2023

Monday 14

Tuesday 15

Charles Godfrey Leland's Birthday

Wednesday 16

☽V/C 4:37 am
☽♍ 6:14 pm
● New Moon (Micro) 4:38 am

Thursday 17

National Thrift Shop Day
Black Cat Appreciation Day

Friday 18

Bad Poetry Day
Serendipity Day

Saturday 19

☽V/C 3:50 am
☽♎ 6:54 am

Sunday 20

August 21–27

August 2023

Mo	Tu	We	Th	Fr	Sa	Su
	1	2	3	4	5	6
7	8	9	10	11	12	13
14	15	16	17	18	19	20
21	22	23	24	25	26	27
28	29	30	31			

Monday 21

☽V/C 3:30 pm
☽♏ 6:22 pm
National Senior Citizens Day

Tuesday 22

Tooth Fairy Day

Wednesday 23

Ride Like the Wind Day
☉♍ 4:02 am Sun enters Virgo
☿℞ Begins

Thursday 24

Vesuvius Day
☽V/C 12:09 am
☽♐ 3:08 am
National Waffle Day

Friday 25

Saturday 26

☽V/C 6:55 am
☽♑ 8:06 am
Women's Equality Day

Sunday 27

Just Because Day
♄☌☉ Saturn at Opposition and closest to Earth

August 28–September 3

August 2023						
Mo	Tu	We	Th	Fr	Sa	Su
	1	2	3	4	5	6
7	8	9	10	11	12	13
14	15	16	17	18	19	20
21	22	23	24	25	26	27
28	29	30	31			

September 2023						
Mo	Tu	We	Th	Fr	Sa	Su
				1	2	3
4	5	6	7	8	9	10
11	12	13	14	15	16	17
18	19	20	21	22	23	24
25	26	27	28	29	30	

Monday 28

☽V/C 6:48 am
☽≈ 9:32 am

Tuesday 29

☽V/C 10:03 pm

Wednesday 30

♣
☽♓ 8:57 am
○ Full Moon 8:35 pm (Supermoon, Blue Moon)

Thursday 31

Raymond Buckland's Birthday

Friday 1

☽V/C 5:35 am
☽♈ 8:25 am

Saturday 2

Sunday 3

☽V/C 6:56 am
☽♉ 10:00 am

September 4–10

September 2023

Mo	Tu	We	Th	Fr	Sa	Su
				1	2	3
4	5	6	7	8	9	10
11	12	13	14	15	16	17
18	19	20	21	22	23	24
25	26	27	28	29	30	

Monday 4

World Sexual Health Day
Labor Day (U.S. Federal Holiday)

Tuesday 5

☽V/C 11:45 am
☽♊ 3:07 pm

Wednesday 6

Thursday 7

☽V/C 5:21 pm

Friday 8

☽♋ 12:00 am
International Literacy Day

Saturday 9

Sunday 10

☽V/C 7:47 am
☽♌ 11:36 am
National Grandparents Day
Carl Llewellyn Weschcke's Birthday

September 11–17

Mo	Tu	We	Th	Fr	Sa	Su
				1	2	3
4	5	6	7	8	9	10
11	12	13	14	15	16	17
18	19	20	21	22	23	24
25	26	27	28	29	30	

September 2023

Monday 11

Silver RavenWolf's Birthday

Tuesday 12

)V/C 10:05 am

Wednesday 13

)♍ 12:18 am
International Programmers' Day

Thursday 14

● New Moon 8:39 pm

Friday 15

☿℞ Ends
☽V/C 8:49 am
☽♎ 12:45 pm

Saturday 16

Sunday 17

☽V/C 8:06 pm
☽♏ 11:58 pm

September 18–24

September 2023						
Mo	Tu	We	Th	Fr	Sa	Su
				1	2	3
4	5	6	7	8	9	10
11	12	13	14	15	16	17
18	19	20	21	22	23	24
25	26	27	28	29	30	

Monday 18

Tuesday 19

Wednesday 20

☽V/C 5:21 am
☽♐ 9:06 am

Thursday 21

Friday 22

☽V/C 2:31 pm
☽♑ 3:21 pm
☉♎ 11:50 pm Sun enters Libra
❋ Sabbat 11:50 pm: Autumn Equinox/Spring Equinox
☿ Mercury at Greatest Western Elongation,
  view the planet low in the eastern sky just before sunrise.

Saturday 23

Sunday 24

☽V/C 3:05 pm
☽♒ 6:30 pm

September 25–October 1

September 2023						
Mo	Tu	We	Th	Fr	Sa	Su
				1	2	3
4	5	6	7	8	9	10
11	12	13	14	15	16	17
18	19	20	21	22	23	24
25	26	27	28	29	30	

October 2023						
Mo	Tu	We	Th	Fr	Sa	Su
						1
2	3	4	5	6	7	8
9	10	11	12	13	14	15
16	17	18	19	20	21	22
23	24	25	26	27	28	29
30	31					

Monday 25

Tuesday 26

☽V/C 7:38 am
☽⚹ 7:18 pm

Wednesday 27

♣

Thursday 28

☽V/C 3:57 pm
☽♈ 7:18 pm

Friday 29

○ Full Moon (Supermoon) 4:57 am

Saturday 30

☽V/C 4:49 pm
☽♉ 8:18 pm

Sunday 1

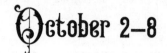 October 2–8

October 2023

Mo	Tu	We	Th	Fr	Sa	Su
						1
2	3	4	5	6	7	8
9	10	11	12	13	14	15
16	17	18	19	20	21	22
23	24	25	26	27	28	29
30	31					

Monday 2

☽V/C 8:19 pm

Tuesday 3

☽Ⅱ 12:03 am

Wednesday 4

Thursday 5

☽V/C 1:34 am
☽♋ 7:32 am

Friday 6

Saturday 7

☽V/C 2:11 pm
☽♌ 6:25 pm
☄ Draconids Meteor Shower

Sunday 8

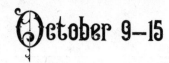

October 2023

Mo	Tu	We	Th	Fr	Sa	Su
						1
2	3	4	5	6	7	8
9	10	11	12	13	14	15
16	17	18	19	20	21	22
23	24	25	26	27	28	29
30	31					

Monday 9

Indigenous People's Day (U.S. Federal Holiday)

Tuesday 10

☽V/C 4:36 am
☽♍ 7:02 am

Wednesday 11

Thursday 12

☽V/C 3:10 pm
☽♎ 7:22 pm

Friday 13

Saturday 14

● New Moon 12:55 pm
12:59 pm Annular Solar Eclipse

Sunday 15

☽V/C 2:00 am
☽♏ 6:04 am

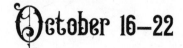 October 16–22

		October 2023				
Mo	Tu	We	Th	Fr	Sa	Su
						1
2	3	4	5	6	7	8
9	10	11	12	13	14	15
16	17	18	19	20	21	22
23	24	25	26	27	28	29
30	31					

Monday 16

Tuesday 17

☽V/C 10:43 am
☽♐ 2:37 pm

Wednesday 18

Thursday 19

☽V/C 2:01 pm
☽♑ 8:55 pm

Friday 20

☿☌☉ 12:49 am Mercury Solar Conjunction

Saturday 21

Orionid Meteor Shower

Sunday 22

☽V/C 1:00 am
☽♒ 1:06 am
Orionid Meteor Shower

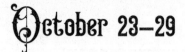 October 23–29

Mo	Tu	We	Th	Fr	Sa	Su
October 2023						
						1
2	3	4	5	6	7	8
9	10	11	12	13	14	15
16	17	18	19	20	21	22
23	24	25	26	27	28	29
30	31					

Monday 23

☽ V/C 2:04 pm
☉ ♏ 11:21 am Sun enters Scorpio
♀ Venus at Greatest Western Elongation,
   view the planet low in the eastern sky just before sunrise.

Tuesday 24

☽ ♓ 3:33 am

Wednesday 25

♣

Thursday 26

☽ V/C 1:38 am
☽ ♈ 5:02 am

Friday 27

Saturday 28

☽ V/C 3:19 am
☽ ♉ 6:44 am
○ Full Moon 3:24 pm
3:14 pm Partial Lunar Eclipse

Sunday 29

October 30—November 5

| | October 2023 | | | | | |
Mo	Tu	We	Th	Fr	Sa	Su
						1
2	3	4	5	6	7	8
9	10	11	12	13	14	15
16	17	18	19	20	21	22
23	24	25	26	27	28	29
30	31					

| | November 2023 | | | | | |
Mo	Tu	We	Th	Fr	Sa	Su
	1	2	3	4	5	
6	7	8	9	10	11	12
13	14	15	16	17	18	19
20	21	22	23	24	25	26
27	28	29	30			

Monday 30

☽V/C 6:35 am
☽♊ 10:08 am

Tuesday 31

❀ Sabbat: Samhain/Beltane

Wednesday 1

☽V/C 7:36 am
☽♋ 4:31 pm

Thursday 2

♃☌☉ 11:55 pm Jupiter at opposition

Friday 3

☽V/C 10:27 pm
♃☌☉ Jupiter at Opposition and closest to Earth

Saturday 4

☽♌ 2:21 am
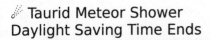 Taurid Meteor Shower

Sunday 5

 Taurid Meteor Shower
Daylight Saving Time Ends

November 6–12

Mo	Tu	We	Th	Fr	Sa	Su
		1	2	3	4	5
6	7	8	9	10	11	12
13	14	15	16	17	18	19
20	21	22	23	24	25	26
27	28	29	30			

November 2023

Monday 6

☽V/C 1:25 am
☽♍ 1:39 pm

Tuesday 7

⊗ Exact Cross-Quarter 10:18 am: Samhain/Beltane

Wednesday 8

☽V/C 10:54 pm

Thursday 9

☽︎♎︎ 2:08 am

Friday 10

Veterans Day Observed (U.S. Federal Holiday)

Saturday 11

☽︎V/C 9:05 am
☽︎♏︎ 12:39 pm
Veterans Day

Sunday 12

 Taurid Meteor Shower

November 13–19

November 2023

Mo	Tu	We	Th	Fr	Sa	Su
		1	2	3	4	5
6	7	8	9	10	11	12
13	14	15	16	17	18	19
20	21	22	23	24	25	26
27	28	29	30			

Monday 13

☽V/C 5:03 pm
☽♐ 8:23 pm
● New Moon 3:27 am

Tuesday 14

Wednesday 15

☽V/C 4:56 pm

Thursday 16

☽♑ 1:42 am

Friday 17

☄ Leonid Meteor Shower
♂☌☉ Mars at Solar Conjunction

Saturday 18

☽V/C 2:27 am
☽♒ 5:28 am
☄ Leonid Meteor Shower

Sunday 19

November 20–26

November 2023

Mo	Tu	We	Th	Fr	Sa	Su
		1	2	3	4	5
6	7	8	9	10	11	12
13	14	15	16	17	18	19
20	21	22	23	24	25	26
27	28	29	30			

Monday 20

☽V/C 4:49 am
☽⯰ 8:29 am

Tuesday 21

♣

Wednesday 22

☽V/C 9:09 am
☽♈ 11:20 am
☉♐ 8:03 am Sun enters Sagittarius

Thursday 23

Thanksgiving Day (U.S. Federal Holiday)

Friday 24

☽V/C 11:40 am
☽♉ 2:29 pm

Saturday 25

Sunday 26

☽V/C 3:51 pm
☽♊ 6:40 pm

November 27–December 3

Mo	Tu	We	Th	Fr	Sa	Su
		1	2	3	4	5
6	7	8	9	10	11	12
13	14	15	16	17	18	19
20	21	22	23	24	25	26
27	28	29	30			

November 2023

Mo	Tu	We	Th	Fr	Sa	Su
				1	2	3
4	5	6	7	8	9	10
11	12	13	14	15	16	17
18	19	20	21	22	23	24
25	26	27	28	29	30	31

December 2023

Monday 27

○ Full Moon 3:16 am

Tuesday 28

☽ V/C 7:02 pm

Wednesday 29

☽ ♋ 12:54 am

Thursday 30

Friday 1

☽V/C 7:06 am
☽♌ 10:01 am

Saturday 2

Sunday 3

☽V/C 8:11 pm
☽♍ 9:50 pm

December 4–10

December 2023

Mo	Tu	We	Th	Fr	Sa	Su
				1	2	3
4	5	6	7	8	9	10
11	12	13	14	15	16	17
18	19	20	21	22	23	24
25	26	27	28	29	30	31

Monday 4

☿ Mercury at Greatest Eastern Elongation
   view the planet low in the western sky just after sunset.

Tuesday 5

Wednesday 6

☽V/C 7:49 am
☽♎ 10:35 am

Thursday 7

Friday 8

☽V/C 7:05 pm
☽♏ 9:35 pm

Saturday 9

Sunday 10

December 11–17

Mo	Tu	We	Th	Fr	Sa	Su
				1	2	3
4	5	6	7	8	9	10
11	12	13	14	15	16	17
18	19	20	21	22	23	24
25	26	27	28	29	30	31

December 2023

Monday 11

☽V/C 2:57 am
☽✗ 5:11 am

Tuesday 12

● New Moon 5:32 pm

Wednesday 13

☽V/C 12:48 am
☽♑ 9:32 am
☿℞ Begins

Thursday 14

🌠 Geminid Meteor Shower

Friday 15

☽V/C 10:03 am
☽♒ 11:56 am
Friday Gladheart's Birthday

Saturday 16

♣

Sunday 17

☽V/C 6:03 am
☽♓ 1:59 pm

December 18–24

December 2023

Mo	Tu	We	Th	Fr	Sa	Su
				1	2	3
4	5	6	7	8	9	10
11	12	13	14	15	16	17
18	19	20	21	22	23	24
25	26	27	28	29	30	31

Monday 18

Tuesday 19

☽V/C 3:03 pm
☽♈ 4:47 pm

Wednesday 20

Thursday 21

☽V/C 8:46 pm
☽♉ 8:50 pm
☄ Ursid Meteor Shower
☉♑ 9:27 pm Sun enters Capricorn
❈ Sabbat 9:27 pm: Winter Solstice/Summer Solstice

Friday 22

☄ Ursid Meteor Shower
☽☌♃ 8:24 am Conjunction of the Moon and Jupiter

Saturday 23

Sunday 24

☽V/C 12:39 am
☽♊ 2:15 am

December 25–31

December 2023

Mo	Tu	We	Th	Fr	Sa	Su
				1	2	3
4	5	6	7	8	9	10
11	12	13	14	15	16	17
18	19	20	21	22	23	24
25	26	27	28	29	30	31

Monday 25

Christmas Day (U.S. Federal Holiday)

Tuesday 26

☽V/C 1:55 am
☽♋ 9:15 am
○ Full Moon 6:33 pm

Wednesday 27

Thursday 28

☽V/C 4:57 pm
☽♌ 6:23 pm
National Card Playing Day

Friday 29

Saturday 30

☽V/C 11:18 pm

Sunday 31

♣
☽♍ 5:54 am

Monthly Planner Worksheets

●●●●●●●●●◐◐○○○○○○○○○◑◑●◐◑●●●●●

Monthly planners pages help you visualize moon phases quickly and are handy for scheduling energy work, magic, and spells. When you work with the correspondences for the days of the week and the phases of the moon, the monthly planner pages help you find any given day within a specific moon phase. For example, if you want to cast a spell on a Friday during the waxing moon, you'll see that Friday, February 3, fulfills this requirement. You can also use these planners to track your cycles, energy levels, pet medications, or monthly tasks. The columns on the right have sections for you to take notes about the moon phases.

A Note on Fertility & Cycle Tracking Apps

The medical privacy laws of HIPAA do not cover the information you store in digital cycle tracking apps. The companies that provide these apps are free to use and share data. Even when a company's privacy policy states that they will not share your information, there is no guarantee that they will adhere to that policy. Additionally, companies will usually comply with court subpoenas demanding information. The FTC cited one popular cycle-tracking app for sharing data from over 100 million users with Facebook even though their policy stated they would not do so. Companies might choose to sell data when the profits from doing so are higher than the fines from the FTC.

It may be necessary to begin tracking cycles non-digitally. On June 24, 2022, the United States Supreme Court overturned the landmark case of Roe vs. Wade, effectively ending the right to abortion by leaving states to decide their laws on the matter. There are now serious concerns across the country regarding access to birth control and other reproductive rights. As extremist religious conservatives have been infiltrating political positions from local town councils and school boards to the senate, they may target birth control next.

Data from cycle tracking apps has not been used to prosecute pregnant people in the U.S. as of August 2022; however, there is already precedence for using data from apps in other prosecutions. Use the monthly planners or other off-line means to ensure your privacy, and please be sure to vote.

January Planner

1	Su	◐		Waxing
2	Mo	◐		
3	Tu	◐		
4	We	◐		
5	Th	○		Full
6	**Fr**	○	Full Moon	
7	Sa	○		
8	Su	○		Waning
9	Mo	◑		
10	Tu	◑		
11	We	◑		
12	Th	◑		
13	Fr	◑		
14	**Sa**	◑		
15	Su	◑		
16	Mo	◑		
17	Tu	◑		
18	We	◑	☿℞ Ends	
19	Th	◑		
20	Fr	●		New
21	**Sa**	●		
22	Su	●		
23	Mo	●		Waxing
24	Tu	◕		
25	We	◕		
26	Th	◕		
27	Fr	◕		
28	**Sa**	◐		
29	Su	◐		
30	Mo	◐		
31	Tu	◐		

February Planner

1	We	◐		Waxing
2	Th	◐ ❀		
3	Fr	◐ ⊕		
4	Sa	◯		Full
5	**Su**	◯	Full Moon	
6	Mo	◯		
7	Tu	◯		Waning
8	We	◯		
9	Th	◑		
10	Fr	◑		
11	Sa	◑		
12	Su	◑		
13	**Mo**	◑		
14	Tu	◑		
15	We	◐		
16	Th	◐		
17	Fr	◐		
18	Sa	◐		
19	Su	●		New
20	**Mo**	●		
21	Tu	●		
22	We	●		Waxing
23	Th	◐		
24	Fr	◐		
25	Sa	◐		
26	Su	◐		
27	**Mo**	◐		
28	Tu	◐		

March Planner

1	We	◑	Waxing
2	Th	◐	
3	Fr	◐	
4	Sa	○	
5	Su	○	
6	Mo	○	Full
7	**Tu**	○ Full Moon	
8	We	○	
9	Th	○	Waning
10	Fr	◗	
11	Sa	◗	
12	Su	◗ DST Begins	
13	Mo	◗	
14	**Tu**	◖	
15	We	◖	
16	Th	◖	
17	Fr	◖	
18	Sa	●	
19	Su	●	
20	**Mo**	● ❀ Equinox	New
21	**Tu**	●	
22	**We**	●	
23	Th	●	Waxing
24	Fr	●	
25	Sa	◐	
26	Su	◐	
27	Mo	◐	
28	**Tu**	◑	
29	We	◑	
30	Th	◐	
31	Fr	○	

April Planner

1	Sa	◐		Waxing
2	Su	◐		
3	Mo	◯		
4	Tu	◯		Full
5	**We**	◯ Full Moon		
6	Th	◯		
7	Fr	◯		Waning
8	Sa	◯		
9	Su	◗		
10	Mo	◗		
11	Tu	◗		
12	We	◗		
13	**Th**	◑		
14	Fr	◑		
15	Sa	◑		
16	Su	◕		
17	Mo	◕		
18	Tu	●		New
19	**We**	●		
20	Th	●		
21	Fr	●	☿℞ Begins	Waxing
22	Sa	●		
23	Su	◑		
24	Mo	●		
25	Tu	◑		
26	We	◐		
27	**Th**	◐		
28	Fr	◐		
29	Sa	◐		
30	Su	◯		

May Planner

1	Mo	☽ ❉	Waxing
2	Tu	☽	
3	We	☽	
4	Th	☽	Full
5	**Fr**	☽ ⊕Full Moon	
6	Sa	☽	
7	Su	☽	Waning
8	Mo	☽	
9	Tu	☽	
10	We	☽	
11	Th	☽	
12	Fr	☽	
13	**Sa**	☽	
14	Su	☽ ☿℞ Ends	
15	Mo	☽	
16	Tu	☽	
17	We	☽	
18	Th	●	New
19	**Fr**	●	
20	Sa	●	
21	Su	●	Waxing
22	Mo	●	
23	Tu	●	
24	We	●	
25	Th	●	
26	Fr	◐	
27	**Sa**	◐	
28	Su	◐	
29	Mo	◐	
30	Tu	◐	
31	We	◐	

June Planner

1	Th	◖		Waxing
2	Fr	◖		Full
3	**Sa**	◯	Full Moon	
4	Su	◯		
5	Mo	◯		Waning
6	Tu	◯		
7	We	◗		
8	Th	◗		
9	Fr	◗		
10	**Sa**	◗		
11	Su	◑		
12	Mo	◑		
13	Tu	◑		
14	We	●		
15	Th	●		
16	Fr	●		New
17	**Sa**	●		
18	Su	●		
19	Mo	●		Waxing
20	Tu	●		
21	We	◕	❄Solstice	
22	Th	◐		
23	Fr	◐		
24	Sa	◐		
25	Su	◐		
26	**Mo**	◑		
27	Tu	◖		
28	We	◖		
29	Th	◖		
30	Fr	◯		

136

July Planner

1	Sa	◯	Waxing
2	Su	◯	Full
3	**Mo**	◯ Full Moon	
4	Tu	◯	
5	We	◯	Waning
6	Th	◯	
7	Fr	◯	
8	Sa	◑	
9	**Su**	◑	
10	Mo	◑	
11	Tu	◑	
12	We	◑	
13	Th	◑	
14	Fr	●	
15	Sa	●	
16	Su	●	New
17	**Mo**	●	
18	Tu	●	
19	We	●	Waxing
20	Th	●	
21	Fr	◑	
22	Sa	◑	
23	Su	◑	
24	Mo	◑	
25	**Tu**	◑	
26	We	◑	
27	Th	◯	
28	Fr	◯	
29	Sa	◯	
30	Su	◯	
31	Mo	◯	Full

August Planner

1	**Tu**	○ ✳Full Moon	Full
2	We	○	
3	Th	○	Waning
4	Fr	○	
5	Sa	◖	
6	Su	◗	
7	Mo	◗ ⊕	
8	**Tu**	◗	
9	We	◖	
10	Th	◖	
11	Fr	◖	
12	Sa	●	
13	Su	●	
14	Mo	●	
15	Tu	●	New
16	**We**	●	
17	Th	●	
18	Fr	●	Waxing
19	Sa	●	
20	Su	◐	
21	Mo	◐	
22	Tu	◐	
23	We	◐ ☿℞ Begins	
24	**Th**	◐	
25	Fr	◐	
26	Sa	◐	
27	Su	○	
28	Mo	○	
29	Tu	○	Full
30	**We**	○ Full Moon	
31	Th	○	

September Planner

1	Fr	○	Waning
2	Sa	○	
3	Su	○	
4	Mo	◑	
5	Tu	◑	
6	**We**	◑	
7	Th	◑	
8	Fr	◑	
9	Sa	◕	
10	Su	◕	
11	Mo	◕	
12	Tu	◕	
13	We	●	New
14	**Th**	●	
15	Fr	● ☿℞ Ends	
16	Sa	●	Waxing
17	Su	●	
18	Mo	◕	
19	Tu	◑	
20	We	◑	
21	Th	◑	
22	**Fr**	◑ ✺Equinox	
23	Sa	◑	
24	Su	◐	
25	Mo	◐	
26	Tu	○	
27	We	○	
28	Th	○	Full
29	**Fr**	○ Full Moon	
30	Sa	○	

October Planner

1	Su	◐	Waning
2	Mo	◑	
3	Tu	◑	
4	We	◑	
5	Th	◑	
6	**Fr**	◑	
7	Sa	◖	
8	Su	◖	
9	Mo	●	
10	Tu	●	
11	We	●	
12	Th	●	
13	Fr	●	New
14	**Sa**	●	
15	Su	●	
16	Mo	●	Waxing
17	Tu	●	
18	We	●	
19	Th	◗	
20	Fr	◗	
21	**Sa**	◑	
22	Su	◑	
23	Mo	◖	
24	Tu	◯	
25	We	◯	
26	Th	◯	
27	Fr	◯	Full
28	**Sa**	◯ Full Moon	
29	Su	◯	
30	Mo	◯	Waning
31	Tu	◑ ✾	

November Planner

1	We	○	Waning
2	Th	○	
3	Fr	○	
4	Sa	○	
5	**Su**	◐ DST Ends	
6	Mo	◐	
7	Tu	◐ ⊕	
8	We	◑	
9	Th	●	
10	Fr	●	
11	Sa	●	
12	Su	●	New
13	**Mo**	●	
14	Tu	●	
15	We	●	Waxing
16	Th	●	
17	Fr	●	
18	Sa	●	
19	Su	◑	
20	**Mo**	◑	
21	Tu	◑	
22	We	◯	
23	Th	◯	
24	Fr	○	
25	Sa	○	
26	Su	○	Full
27	**Mo**	○ Full Moon	
28	Tu	○	
29	We	◐	Waning
30	Th	○	

December Planner

1	Fr	◯	Waning
2	Sa	◑	
3	Su	◑	
4	**Mo**	◑	
5	Tu	◑	
6	We	◑	
7	Th	◑	
8	Fr	◑	
9	Sa	●	
10	Su	●	
11	Mo	●	New
12	**Tu**	●	
13	We	●	☿℞ Begins
14	Th	●	Waxing
15	Fr	●	
16	Sa	◐	
17	Su	◐	
18	Mo	◐	
19	**Tu**	◐	
20	We	◐	
21	Th	◐	❀Solstice
22	Fr	◯	
23	Sa	◯	
24	Su	◯	
25	Mo	◯	Full
26	**Tu**	◯	Full Moon
27	We	◯	
28	Th	◯	
29	Fr	◯	
30	Sa	◑	
31	Su	◑	

Infinite Spells

This year's theme is all about you being able to create a spell for any purpose. You'll learn the fundamentals of spell design and how to apply your creativity and intuition to your workings.

Creating Your Own Spells

A spell does not have to come from an ancient text in order for it to be powerful and effective. In fact, these archaic spells are often fragmented, antiquated, and obsolete. Modern spells are based on the framework of traditional spell design but may also incorporate science and psychology.

Gratitude rituals can be used as an example of modern spell design. Such rituals involve focusing on the blessings that surround you and letting yourself be imbued with gratitude.

Focusing on being grateful has been shown to improve physical and psychological health and boost happiness. In recent studies, the essential oil of helichrysum has shown promise in lessening anxiety and depression. A modern spell for happiness might include a yellow candle (traditional color correspondence), a gratitude ritual (psychological studies), and an anointing oil made with helichrysum (scientific studies). The book of shadows template on page 191 shows you a record of a gratitude ritual utilizing these elements.

As you learn the fundamentals of magic you'll be able to recognize a well-designed spell. Such spells should resonate with you and follow the basic magical principles of sympathetic magic. They should also trigger your mind to enhance your focus and visualization.

Every well-designed spell has the potential to be powerful, but the power comes from you, not the spell. Self confidence, a focused mind, a positive attitude, a strong will, and clear intentions will help ensure your success. Spells are simply tools.

Compare a spell to a common tool such as a hammer. A hammer alone is not powerful but when wielded by a person it can be a tool of creation or destruction. The intentions of the person using the hammer determine the results of its use. The person using the hammer is the source of the power, the hammer simply focuses their energy in a specific way.

There are well designed spells available in many books and websites. Using these spells is a good place to start however, you empower yourself by creating your own spells. It is better to use these ready-made spells as inspiration for your own designs. A spell you create is always going to be the best spell for you. Your energy is more closely connected to the work because it came from you and is tailored to fit your exact intentions. Every time you design and implement a spell you learn more about yourself and magic, and your skills grow.

The following pages will show you how to create a spell for any occasion. You might start with a simple candle spell and explore other tools and ingredients to refine your focus. Remember that you are the most important component in spell-work and all the other accouterments should be included only to assist your focus, not as distractions.

Define Your Goal

A spell begins the moment you decide to cast one. Planning the design and collecting the ingredients are all part of the actual spell. But before you begin all of that, consider your real goal. Casting a spell for money to get a car is limiting the ways in which that car can manifest in your life. It is better to cast a spell for a car. Ask yourself probing questions and be honest and objective. Do I need friends or lovers or do I need self-confidence? Do I need another job or am I living beyond my means or keeping myself busy to avoid something at home? Make sure that your spell is focused on your goal and is *result oriented*, not *method oriented*. Consult some form of divination such as tarot cards, oracle cards, or runes to help you reflect on your goal.

Perform Divination

You might try reading your tea leaves before casting a spell. If you've never done this before, instructions begin on page 193. You may also draw a few tarot cards, oracle cards, or runes to gain some final insights about your spell. You can use any layout such as those on page 188, or try this one:

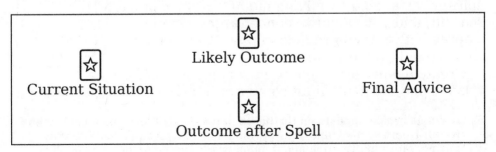

Design Your Spell

Knowing yourself is a big part of what type of spell you will design to help you focus. Consider how much time you have, your budget, and what types of things you associate with your goal. Use the following pages to help you find ingredients, suggestions, and techniques to help in your design.

Find Your Work Space

You will need some privacy for casting spells. Find a place where you won't be disturbed and where you feel comfortable. You don't need a ritual room or even a formal altar to work magic. You can cast a spell in a park, your bathroom, or on the kitchen counter.

You can use the ground or floor for your work surface, and you might consider obtaining a special meditation pillow to make sitting more comfortable. Ideally you would have a small table or flat-topped box where you can store supplies such as candles, herbs, or ritual tools.

Prepare Your Setting

Set up everything you need to cast your spell. Don't forget matches or a lighter if you are using candles or incense. Whenever you are burning something, work in a ventilated area that isn't directly under a smoke detector.

Just as you cleared your mind in preparation for your spell, clear your workspace and set the mood. A good physical cleaning and decluttering is appropriate, and a smoke cleansing or psychic clearing is a good idea.

Practical witches might combine physical and spiritual cleansing by mixing moon water[5], a pinch of sea salt, and your favorite concentrated cleaner into a spray bottle. While you clean physically, focus on clearing out baneful energies.

Create a clear atmosphere in which you can feel relaxed and magical. Light some candles, burn some purification

Moon Water

Alcohol

Vinegar

---

5   A simple recipe appears on the bottle in the illustration. Use 4 parts moon water, 1 part alcohol, and 2 parts vinegar. Add a pinch of sea salt after mixing. More information about moon water can be found on page 209.

incense, lower the lights, and otherwise set the stage. You might feel more witchy when you wear a special ritual cloak, or maybe you like to have all of your Wiccan tools set up on your altar. Whatever setting you prefer, make it yours. Double check that you have everything you need for your spell and have selected a good time for casting. Working with the phases of the moon and the days of the week will incorporate natural energies and traditional correspondences into your spell. More importantly is a finding a time when you are rested and clear-headed.

Enter Your Magical Mindset

Before you begin to work any magic you must enter a proper state of mind. If you begin your spell out of desperation you will only add that energy to the working. Your objective is to be relaxed, confident, and positive.

Preparing your setting for magic as previously mentioned will begin to trigger this mindset, but now that everything is ready it is time to finish preparing yourself.

Sit comfortably and release any self defeating thoughts fears, doubts, and insecurities. Set aside distracting thoughts and breathe slowly and deeply. Relax until the mental clutter is gone. Take your time and know that with experience you will achieve a relaxed state quickly.

Now that your mind is clear of mundane thoughts and you are relaxed, reaffirm that you are ready for your will and desire to manifest. Know that your goal is a reality for you. Affirm that you are ready and deserving of achieving that goal.

Continue deep, steady breaths until you feel as if you are entering a daydream-like state of relaxation. Magic flows best at that time right before you fall asleep when alpha waves are prevalent in your brain wave patterns.

Cast Your Spell

Breathe deeply and re-affirm your goal. Cast a circle (if you do so for your magic) and perform your spell.

Keep a Record

Your magical journal or book of shadows (bos) is an important part of successful magic. Record your divination sessions, spells, thoughts, magical correspondences, or whatever else you feel is important. Referring back to previous bos entries gives you insight into what works best for you.

You are the only tool you need to perform magic but, your bos is probably the second most important. It is a direct reflection of you and your craft, a record of your experiences and insights, and a journal for exploring your inner self.

There are many digital options such as LiberOffice, JRNL, Sol Journal, GitJournal, mobile apps, and others. You might save your bos as one long file or many smaller files. When using digital formats, be sure to save and backup frequently.

There are also many physical formats for your bos. A book with sewn-in pages may not suit a perfectionist because mistakes are hard to remove. You might prefer a post-bound scrapbook or a three-ring binder (often referred to as a spell-binder). You can use anything you like and make it fancy or modest. Eventually you may have several bos in your collection.

Whether digital or physical, **it is essential that you choose a format that you will use.** Record your spellwork in your bos immediately after your workings while the experiences are fresh in your mind. This simple act can help you ground after magic and rituals. Remember to go back later and take notes about the results of your spells after some time has passed.

Many psychologists recommend journaling by hand as a cognitive exercise. It requires your brain to connect with specific parts of your mind, known in psychology as the *reading circuit*. If you use a digital version you can mimic the physical act of writing with a stylus. Although this is not necessary, Gardnerian and Alexandrian traditions of witchcraft require adherence to the Ardanes. These Ardanes are purportedly old laws passed down through the generations. One such Ardane is *"if you would keep a book, let it be in your own hand of write."* Some adherents to these traditions interpret this as the physical act of writing while others interpret it as *"in your own words."*

Physical versions are not necessarily superior to digital versions so use what works best for you.

A book of shadows sample page is on page 191 with an example gratitude spell recorded in gray. You can use this sample template for your bos or design your own.

Spell Construction

Sympathetic Magic

Sympathetic magic is used to some degree in every faith and culture in the world. People have built a variety of practices based on the two main principles of sympathetic magic; the **Law of Similarities** and the **Law of Contagion**. Understanding these two principles makes it easier for you to design spells.

Law of Similarities

This is the magical principle of "like attracts like". Similarities are often in the form of imitation such as a when a poppet or photograph is used in a spell. Similarities are also used through correspondences. When we use plants, stones, and other items that are associated with certain traits we are using the Law of Similarity through correspondences.

Law of Contagion

This is the principle that two things that have been in contact with each other remain linked because the magical essence of each is imbued into the other. Think of it like the transfer of molecules when two people or things come into contact, or the transfer of fingerprints left on items.

Traditional Elemental Correspondences

An easy way to work with the principle of similarity is to use elemental correspondences. The classical elements of earth, air, fire, and water rose from the teachings of ancient Greek philosophers. The elemental correspondences of botanicals then developed from Greek and Roman medical texts along with writings from India and Tibet.

The development of these correspondences were perpetuated in Medieval grimoires and were further developed by Renaissance philosophers. Hermetic traditions and the Golden Dawn adopted and refined these correspondences throughout the 19th and 20th centuries. By the mid 20th, century, these concepts had been incorporated into Gardnerian Wicca. Later, these concepts were adopted by many New Age traditions. Scott Cunningham's correspondence books sold well in the magical communities in the 1990s and have become standard reference material. He used many resources to create his correspondences, but especially relied upon the works of Nicholas Culpeper[6] and the Golden Dawn.

It is important to consider that traditional correspondences were recorded by upper class men who were more familiar with books than with plants. They had a reductive approach to nature and combined Greek philosophy with the Bible and other Abrahamic religious texts. Village wise women, farmers, and practitioners of folk magic were not writing books about magic during most of the development of correspondences.

By using the traditional correspondences, you are tapping into a *collective energy* source. This well of energy can be drawn from because so many people have shared the same correspondences and associations for so long.

Maybe you've heard of the story of the five monkeys. This fictional tale can be seen as an allegory for magical correspondence. Five monkeys are put into a habitat where bananas are suspended above a ladder. One money tries to climb the ladder to get the bananas and is sprayed with water. The next monkey attempts to reach the bananas with the same negative result.

Soon all the monkeys have made their attempts to get the bananas and the same thing always happens. A few new monkeys are then introduced into the habitat and are taught not to attempt to reach the bananas by the original monkeys who were sprayed. Slowly members of the original group are removed and replaced by new members until all that remain are monkeys who have never attempted to reach the bananas. The remaining monkeys never again make the attempt even long after the original monkeys who were reprimanded are removed from the habitat. Like the elemental and planetary correspondences, it is this way because it has always been so.

But you can't precisely rely on the elemental correspondences as they can be fickle. Sea salt is an excellent example of this. Salt is usually attributed to the element of earth. Virtually all salt (NaCl) found on earth originally formed in ancient oceans. Therefore salt corresponds to both earth and water.

Many of the traditional correspondence can seem rather arbitrary. You could easily argue that all botanicals are of earth, and the essence of all four elements are present in every living thing. A dandelion can easily be seen as corresponding with any of the

---

6   Nicholas Culpeper advocated planetary "rulers" of botanicals and grouped plants based on traits of Roman Goddesses and Gods. He is one of the major sources of modern planetary and deity correspondences in magic as is evident in his 1652 book, *The English Physitian* (now sold under the title *Culpeper's Complete Herbal*).

four elements. The roots for earth, golden flowers for fire, puffy seed heads for air, and leaves for water.

Although traditional correspondences do carry *collective energy* is important that you choose spell components primarily based on your intuition and personal associations. Your spell ingredients must resonate with you so that they speak to your subconscious.

Modern Elemental Correspondences

Using traditional correspondences is a good place to start, but your own associations are far more powerful and reliable. They will resonated best with you and speak to your subconscious. You can include your correspondences in your bos or use the worksheet at the end of the correspondences section of your almanac.

A willow tree is a good example to use for modern correspondences. It is traditionally associated with grief and death. This is probably because it was planted in areas with a high water table to keep the ground dry. This was especially done in cemeteries and near churches.

But maybe a willow tree is not "weeping" so much as she is a fountain of playfulness and comfort. Didn't you ever want to swing on her branches? Have you hidden within her trusses while imagining you are inside your own green castle? Have you ever been sad and sat beneath a willow? She can be a source of joy and comfort! Perhaps instead of the correspondence to death and grief she means comfort and healing for you.

The modern approach is to consider the traditional correspondences but select **items which you can easily obtain and that resonate with you**. Imagine that you are looking for a botanical that represents fire in your spell. You note that there are many listed in your almanac, but the one that stands out for you is chili pepper. You have it in the kitchen and both the color and its physical effects remind you of fire.

Let your own associations come first, but try using the traditional correspondences to fill in the gaps and help connect to that collective energy.

Kitchen Witchery Example

Say you have a friend who is having a difficult menstruation. She says that is feeling 'washed out' and lonely. You consider ways in which you might bring her some comfort and remember your aunt used to make some wonderful cookies called *snickerdoodles*. Your own correspondence of snickerdoodles is that of comfort. You decide to put together a care package of practical and magical items with chocolate, movies, and homemade snick-erdoodles.

These cookies contain cinnamon, which you know corresponds to the element of fire. When you add the cinnamon to the recipe you draw on this correspondence and focus your intent while saying "may cinnamon help rekindle her inner fire". You then add some ground up chamomile to the recipe to help soothe cramps and bring in emotional balance.[7]

Combining Correspondences & Elements

Remember to allow your creativity to flow while keeping the traditional correspondences in mind. We'll look at several examples of spells and recipes to inspire you, but let's start with some that use the four elements to work with sympathetic magic.

Elemental Home Buyer's Spell

You've visited the perfect home during an open house event and want to cast a spell to increase your chances of getting the house. The spell you are casting is for attraction and drawing, so you'll want to work during the waxing moon. Thursday and Friday are both good days to cast spells involving money, success, and home. You check your almanac and decide on Friday, October 20th as your spell casting date.

Looking over the correspondences of herbs, oils, and incense, nothing resonates quite right. You decide to re-visit the house and collect a small pinch of dirt from the back yard (earth element and contagion principle). You fill a small vial with water from the house's kitchen tap (water/contagion).

The upstairs linen closet is lined with cedar and you decide to use cedar incense for the air element (and similarity principle). For fire, you select a yellow candle that is the same color as the exterior paint (similarity).

Ritual Purification Incense

To make a purification incense for smoke clearing before magic, look through the elemental correspondences for botanicals. Rosemary is associated with fire, thyme with water, mugwort with earth, and lavender with air. All of these also correspond to purification and cleansing.

Burn a little of each one on a charcoal incense disk to find which ones smell best and remind you of purification. Perhaps

---

7   A snickerdoodle recipe is included in your almanac on page 211.

the scent of frankincense or another botanical evokes a sense of purity and magic in you, so you could include that in your recipe. Your final formula will have more of the things you like, and just a pinch of botanicals you are using for their element. An example using the simpler's method with parts by volume is 1 pt. thyme, 1 pt. lavender, 2 pt. rosemary, 2 pt. mugwort, 4 pt. frankincense.[8]

Spell Timing

Only you can determine the best time for you to cast a spell. Your schedule, energy level, and mood play the most important role in your spell timing. Cast spells when you are feeling energetic and positive.

Try to work with the natural energy of the phases of the moon as described on page 177. You might also experiment with working on days of the week that correspond to your goals as outlined on page 178.

Attract, Repel, Balance

When you begin designing spells keep in mind the overall energy of the working. Start simply with one of the three major energies before you design more complex and intricate spells.

Attracting & Drawing

The correspondence tables in the back include the three primary forms of drawing magic as symbolized below.

❤	Love, Lust, Friendship
$	Money & Prosperity
♣	Luck & Good Fortune

---

8   The simpler's method uses parts (pt.) for scalable recipes. A part is whatever volume or weight measurement you desire such as a pinch or gram.

Repelling & Shielding

The correspondence tables also show the two primary forms of repelling and shielding magic as symbolized below.

☂	Protection & Warding
⚡	Cleansing, Purification & Banishing

Neutral & Balancing

Neutral forms of magic neither push something away nor pull something closer. The two major types are listed thusly.

☽	Dream, Visions, Astral Travel & Divination
☤	Health, Healing, Peace, Harmony

Complex Spell Design

Simple spells are perfectly sufficient to help you manifest your goals, and you don't need to delve into more complex workings. However, working with attraction and repelling in the same spell can be an interesting way to explore your power and the nuances of your magic.

Complex spells require a sharply focused mind. You may want to spend some time practicing simple spells until you feel confident that you can change your mental focus quickly.

After you've practiced the three primary energies of spellwork as outlined on the previous page, you can begin to combine these energies to form subtle and precise spells, such as the example below. For this spell, we'll be utilizing many of the topics covered to this point.

Spell to Change Baneful Habits

Timing

On May 5[9], 2023, the full moon becomes eclipsed[9]. Use this opportunity to work with the natural energies of the waning and then waxing power of the moon.

The eclipse begins at 10:14 am Central Time, but doesn't peak until 12:22 pm. Estimate how long it takes to gather your will and focus on your intentions based on previous spell casting experience. You may want to begin this spell around noon, giving yourself about 20 minutes to focus on banishing baneful habits and thought patterns. Expect to be finished by around 1:00 pm as the eclipse ends, providing you with an hour to work.

Looking at the Moon Sign Magic table on page 179 you'll notice that the moon in Scorpio is a good time for personal growth, change, and exploring your shadows. Use this energy as the eclipse begins to explore bad habits you wish to release and affirm new thought patterns for personal growth.

May 5th is on a Friday, which is conducive to rebirth. Use this energy as the moon waxes to strengthen new thought patterns.

Waning Energy Banishing

Burn a banishing incense as the eclipse begins. Relax and breathe deep while you turn your focus inward. Think about the behaviors and habits you wish to banish.

Let's use the habit of snacking on junk food in the evening as an example. Think about what triggers this binging. When did this habit begin? What might have caused this habit to start, and what continues to trigger it every evening? What associations and memories do you have with the junk foods you choose? Return in your mind to the last time you overindulged. Were you tired? Stressed? Anxious? Continue probing your motivations and revealing your shadows. As you uncover your triggers, release each one and know that it no longer compels you.

Full Eclipse Balancing

As the eclipse approaches its peak, there is an energy of balance. Extinguish any remaining banishing incense and continue breathing deeply and rhythmically. Reaffirm that you have identified and banished your baneful habits and thought patterns. Relax into the moment and feel the balance within you.

---

9   An eclipse does not need to be visible in your area in order for you to work with eclipse energies.

Waxing Energy Renewal

As the eclipse ends, the light of the moon waxes, and you will switch your focus to renewal and rebirth. Light an incense you associate with new beginnings or blessings. Think of new habits you can use to replace the baneful ones you've banished. If you are using junk food as a reward, perhaps you could replace it with a special herbal tea. Maybe junk food is providing you a sugar rush for extra energy, and your sleep habits may need some fine-tuning.

Visualize upcoming evenings where you are no longer binging and instead feel balanced, confident, and proud of yourself. Imagine yourself performing new, healthier habits. Feel the energy of the new rebirth within you.

Spell Adaptation

The abundance of spells online and in books may inspire you. Feel free to modify these spells to suit your goals better. One of the most popular spells online is for attracting money. The following example is a compilation of dozens of social media memes.

Light a green candle and focus on money coming to you while saying, *Money, money come to me. This is my will, so mote it be.*

Sympathetic magic comes into play with the color correspondence of the green candle for prosperity. The words of power rhyme, so they are easy to remember and speak to the subconscious. However, a quick redesign may help this spell resonate better with you.

You could substitute the candle color if you associate red, gold, or another color with prosperity. Maybe you are looking for a specific job rather than a general money spell. You might rewrite the words to specify this like, *This new job will come to me. This is my will so, mote it be.*

Like most online spells, this one doesn't explain the tools and techniques that make a spell successful. Simply lighting a candle and saying some words won't do the trick. The following section covers some methods and additional tools to help.

Tools & Techniques

There are tools available to help you focus your mind and magic. Some of these tools are techniques rather than items or ingredients. These techniques will sharpen your mental powers and help you focus your magic.

Anointing Candles for Spells

Candle magic is a highly effective method for casting spells. Anoint your candle with oil to prepare it for magical use. Anointing is a method of consecrating your candle to align it with your intention.

You can make or purchase a special anointing oil or use whatever you have on hand. The magical correspondences of your oil should be in harmony with your intention. For example, almonds are associated with luck and prosperity, and you might use almond oil for your anointing oil. Plain olive oil is great for any general use.

You can infuse your oil with corresponding herbs. Continuing the example for prosperity, you might add cinnamon sticks and mint leaves to a small bottle of almond oil and let it steep for a few days. Look for more magical oil recipes on pages 203-207.

How to Anoint Your Candles

Place a drop of oil on your fingertips. Focus on your intention and coat your candle with a thin layer of oil. Add more oil to your fingers as needed.

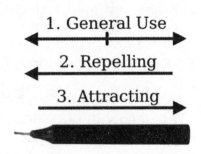

Consider the type of spell you are casting using the general categories on the previous page. Candles for attraction and drawing are usually anointed from top to bottom (3. in the image), representing drawing in or toward you. Candles for repelling and shielding are usually anointed from the bottom to the top (2. in the image), representing energy being pushed out and away. Candles for general use, balanced or neutral spells, or complex spells that involve attracting and repelling are anointed from the center of the candle to the base and then from the center of the candle to the tip.

Container candles and votive cups should be anointed on the top surface around the wick. Apply the oil with your fingertips in a deosil fashion for attracting or general use, and widdershins for repelling and banishing.

Once your candle is coated with a thin layer of oil, you can roll it in finely ground botanicals if you wish. This is usually done when you use a plain anointing oil that has not been infused with herbs or essential oils. Avoid large chunks of botanicals that can catch fire when the candle is burned.

Sigils & Bindrunes

A bindrune is a ligature of two or more runes joined together to form a single glyph. You can create your own bindrune by choosing runes based on your spiritual or magical needs and combining them in creative ways.

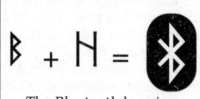

The Bluetooth logo is a bindrune created from Hagall (Hagalaz) and Bjarkan (Berkano)

A sigil is a similar style of ligature created by combining the letters in phrases or keywords that express your intent. There are many methods used to create sigils but the practical technique explained here is very effective.

State your goal with the fewest, most direct words possible. Let's say you want to do a spell for protection. You can use the phrase **I am protected** or simply the word **protection**. Keep your focus on your intent the entire time you create your sigil.

PRØTECTIØN

Eliminate all the vowels in your word or phrase. This results in **prtctn** as shown above. Next, eliminate any repeating letters, in this case the T, which results in **prtcn** as below.

PRØTECTIØN

Use the remaining letters to make a creative glyph. Feel free to rotate letters as desired to suit the vibe of your sigil design. The last sigil in the protection examples on the next page was created using Theban Script which can be found on page 187.

Using Your Sigils & Bindrunes

Sigils can be written on paper, inscribed into the wax of spell-candles, or painted onto stones that correspond to your goal. They can be carried with you as a reminder to focus on your goal throughout the day, or incorporated into spell jars and bags. The following sample spells demonstrate the ways you can use sigils. As you know from the timing section, Thursdays and Sundays during the waxing moon are good for prosperity work.

Prosperity Candle Spell

Anoint your candle moving from the wick to the base or deosil around the wick. Create a sigil for prosperity and carve it into the candle using an athame, boline or toothpick. Burn a small amount of prosperity herbs such as cinnamon, cinquefoil, basil, patchouli, etc. Using the correspondence tables in the back of your almanac; you might choose an herb to represent each of the four elements. You could use the same herbs to infuse the anointing oil for your candle. Rub the ashes from the burnt herbs into the sigil you carved into the candle. Focus your will and intent on your goal as the candle burns.

Prosperity Sigil Release Spell

Create a sigil for prosperity and write it on a piece of paper. You might use a special prosperity ink, watercolor paint, or use ink in a color your associate with prosperity. Gaze at your sigil while focusing your will and intent on your goal. Burn the paper to release your intent into the world where it can manifest.

Prosperity Bottle, Bag, or Box

Spell bottles are currently trending, but spell bags are traditionally more common. The container for your spell depends on how you will use or store the spell. Bottles can be bulky in pockets and purses. Spell bags are not as weatherproof for outdoor storage. You can incorporate color correspondence by selecting a container that is appropriate for prosperity to you. Spell bags can be made of colored fabric, boxes can be painted, and bottles can be sealed with wax of the corresponding color.

Place ingredients that correspond to prosperity into the container you have chosen such as:

1 mercury dime. Mercury dimes are often used in spells. They are made of 90% silver and 10% copper, both of which correspond to prosperity along with the obvious money symbolism. Mercury is a Roman god related to financial gain, commerce, and speed.

1 aventurine stone. Aventurine is a green stone whose color corresponds to money. The energy of this stone is said to attract opportunities and success.

1 prosperity sigil.

Hold the container in your hands and focus your will and intent on your goal. You've just made a type of talisman.

Items Around Your Home

You can use many items from around your home for magic. When you wish to incorporate an object, hold it for a few minutes to see how it blends with your energy. Identify how it makes you feel and what thoughts or images it evokes in your mind. An old trinket box might be perfect for a household protection spell. That bit of string in the junk drawer might be perfect for a cord-cutting spell. If an item seems appropriate, but you are not absolutely positive that it will work, just try it! Record your results in your book of shadows, and you are well on your way to expertise.

You only need yourself to work magic, but you may find items such as candles, incense, and other tools helpful in refining your focus. Only you can decide what will blend with your energy, and some experimentation will help you determine what to include in your spells.

Breathing

Throughout your almanac, there are several references to breathing deeply and rhythmically. Magic users often employ what is called box breathing. To do box breathing, inhale through your nose to the count of four. Hold your breath for another count of four, and then exhale through your mouth to the count of four. Wait while you count to four and then repeat the inhale, hold, exhale, wait.

Visualization

Visualization is one of the primary techniques in magic and is vital for manifestation. You can keep your mental powers sharp by regularly engaging in activities that will stimulate your visualization abilities.

A simple exercise is to look at an object near you, close your eyes, and try to visualize it down to the last detail. When you have a good mental image of the object, try making that mental image move or change shape. Practice this technique regularly to help your skills grow rapidly.

Reading and listening to audiobooks will also help hone your visual skills. Try bringing in other senses, such as imagining a cookie and bringing its fragrance and taste to mind.

Spells for Inspiration

Gratitude Ritual

Expressing gratitude has been shown to help you achieve a sense of well-being, balance, and increased energy. Practical spells such as this work through valid psychological techniques and traditional magical principles.

You will be creating a powerfully charged talisman you can carry with you. Once you have completed the spell, your talisman is imbued with power. Holding it will increase your happiness and energy and it can help you to put stressful situations into perspective for better problem-solving.

Timing Your Spell: Begin your spell on the first day of the waxing moon. This is the second day after the new moon and the monthly Planner Pages will help you schedule your working. You'll complete the spell on the full moon.

Select a Talisman: You can use any object that is easily carried such as a stone, crystal, or piece of jewelry.

Charging Your Talisman: Every day, hold the object you have chosen and focus on one thing for which you are grateful. Of course, you may repeat the exercise throughout the day whenever you think of something. If you carry the talisman in your pocket you can just touch it while you focus your intent. Close your eyes and feel the gratitude you have and send it through your hand into the talisman. Don't allow guilt or a sense of indebtedness creep into your thoughts or emotions. This isn't about owing back, it's about true appreciation, acknowledging and accepting.

You may speak words of power or a prayer of thanks to your chosen deities/deity at the end of your energy projection, or just end your focusing session with 'so mote it be' or an affirmation.

On the last day of your spell think about how the energy of the full moon reflects the fullness of your gratitude. You may choose to leave your talisman out under the moonlight overnight. It doesn't matter if it is cloudy, the full moon will still imbue your talisman with energy. If you have selected an item that should not be left outdoors, just leave it on a windowsill or your altar.

Carry your talisman with you whenever you need a mental or spiritual lift. As the year progresses, you may wish to boost the energy of your talisman by repeating your focus during any moon phase. You might discover that making this a daily ritual can be very rewarding.

Candle Spells

These three spells demonstrate how you can use correspondences to design a candle spell for any purpose. Each spell has a stone, suggested words of power, and an anointing oil. The anointing oils can be essential oils or an infused base oil. Recipes for these oils are on pages 203-207.

While you are gathering your power and focusing your mind, you can inscribe a sigil into the wax of the candle if you like. Note that the protection spell is a repelling energy and should be timed during the waning moon. The attraction and prosperity spells are drawing and should be cast during the waxing moon.

Protection Spell	Attraction Spell	Prosperity Spell
Black Candle Rosemary Oil	Pink or Red Candle Lavender Oil	Green Candle Mint Oil
I hereby banish bane and harm, and protect my realm with this charm.	*Come to me who is meant to be. Let this cause no harm nor turn on me.*	*Abundance flows to me. This is my will, so mote it be.*

Spell Jars & Bags

Spell jars and bags are created in the same manner. The vessel is cleansed with smoke from incense or herbs which correspond to the working. Next, ingredients are added to help refine and focus the energy. The resulting talisman is then carried with you or stored in your home.

Protection & Warding Jar or Bag

This spell uses four ingredients that correspond to each of the four elements. These ingredients all correspond to protection. An additional item that represents you or what you wish to protect is the final fifth ingredient.
- **Earth**: Black Tourmaline
- **Air**: Pine Needles
- **Fire**: Rosemary
- **Water**: Willow
- **The fifth ingredient** can be soil from around a home you wish to protect, a bit of your hair or nail clippings, or a charm that has a special meaning to you. Note how these choices incorporate similarity and contagion.

Burn some incense or herbs corresponding to protection such as rosemary, sage, or sandalwood. Fill the jar or bag with the smoke. Add each ingredient as you focus on your intent. You may say words of power and visualize a sphere emanating from the jar. As you add more ingredients this sphere grows larger and stronger. Because this is a repelling and shielding talisman, it should be created during the waning moon.

Money Jar or Bag

Using the correspondence tables in your almanac, consider which ingredients you would use to attract money. You might use a green bag to incorporate color correspondences, and your ingredients might be:
- **Earth**: Seeds or Oats
- **Air**: Dandelion
- **Fire**: Cinnamon
- **Water**: Violet
- **The fifth ingredient** could be your hair, a piece of a business card from a business where you wish to work, a mercury dime you inherited, etc.

Your incense might be patchouli, cinnamon, or vanilla. You'll be working with attraction so you'll create this during the waxing moon.

Potion Brewing Spells

The classic witch's brew is a wonderful way to cast a spell. You can brew these potions on the stove top, or scale them down and use a candle warmer.

Cleansing & Purification
Bath, Floor Wash & Room Spray

The examples of spell jars and bags on the previous page used elemental correspondences. This isn't always necessary, but it is a good way to launch your creativity. The focus of this potion is cleansing and purification, and botanicals are chosen solely for this purpose.

This recipe uses the simpler's method. Each 'part' you use can be a pinch, a teaspoon, scoop, etc. This scalable style of recipe allows you to use a small measurement unit for brewing potions in a wax warmer such as the one pictured, or a large measurement unit for big pots on the stove.

I prefer to brew potions for banishing and cleansing on Saturdays during the waning moon. Your monthly Planner Pages make it very easy to find these Saturdays, such as January 14th or September 9th.

Ingredients
- 2 part Rosemary
- 1 part Lemon Balm
- 4 parts Lavender
- 1 part Thyme
- Salt (optional)

Floor Wash Directions
- Fill your cauldron half-way full with water. You can use moon water, spring water, or even tap water. Begin heating the water with low heat.
- Combine your botanicals in a mortar and pestle or bowl and lightly crush them until the pieces are about the size of green pepper seeds.

- Brew your potion for 20-30 minutes while occasionally stirring deosil over low heat. Keep the temperature just under boiling. Focus on your intent while your potion brews.
- Allow your potion to cool enough that you can handle it without scalding.
- Strain your potion through a sieve. Adding a few pinches of sea salt or pink Himalayan salt will boost your potions purification energy. Use your potion as your mop water to cleanse and purify your home. Spent botanicals can be composted.

Room Spray Directions
- Brew your potion as directed for the floor wash.
- After straining it through a sieve, pour it through a fine coffee filter to remove all debris.
- Fill a spray bottle ½ way full of your potion and add a small pinch of salt if desired.
- Fill the spray bottle the rest of the way with rubbing alcohol or a high proof ethyl alcohol (at least 70% alcohol or 140 proof). You can optionally add a few drops of essential oil such as lavender, rosemary or clary sage for a fragrance.
- Use your spray to cleanse rooms just as you would for smoke cleansing.

Purification Bath Directions
- Combine the botanicals in a mortar and pestle or bowl and lightly crush them as directed for the floor wash. Keep your focus on your intent and allow your energy to flow into the herbs.
- Fill reusable cloth bags ½ full of the botanical blend.
- Store bath bags in an airtight container.
- When you are ready to have a purification bath, begin filling your tub with very hot water.
- Put one bag under the water and gently squeeze it a few times to push out trapped air.
- Bring the water to a comfortable temperature, and add any soap or oils you prefer.

Spell Casting Q & A

How do spells work?

Most spells help you harness your own power and natural energies to manifest your intentions. Magic also affects you psychologically to affirm that your intentions are achievable.

How often should I cast spells?

There is no simple answer to this question, but casting a spell for something different every day is going to invite chaos into your life. Imagine throwing a rock into a still pond. Notice the ripples emanating out until they reach the shore. Now throw a handful of rocks into the pond. All of the ripples interact with and counteract each other. Throwing your magic around too much is draining and dilutes your focus.

You might design a spell for a singular purpose that is ongoing. You light a candle and focus your energy and intent every day during a particular moon phase. Because this is actually one spell cast over a period of time, it does not cause the chaos and drain one might experience from casting a bunch of different spells.

Very generally speaking you should stick to one spell a week or less. Keep a close eye on your intentions, mental health, and energy levels to reveal what is right for you.

I've seen spells that incorporate unusual ingredients. Are these items more powerful?

Not necessarily. Spells are recipes designed to blend a variety of energies with your own energy to focus it. If you do not feel comfortable with a component of a spell, omit it! Ultimately it is your energy that you are affecting, so if you don't blend with the ingredients, your spell won't blend with you.

Do the words in a spell (words of power) have to rhyme or be memorized and repeated?

No. Repetition is done to help focus your energy. Sometimes a spell is chanted repeatedly to bring on a meditative state or other altered state of consciousness. These deep mind states can be useful in working magic, however repeated chanting is only one of many ways to achieve them. Flickering candlelight, incense, and quiet focus are also conducive to bringing on these states. Each person will differ in how they best achieve the frame of mind in which their magic works. You will find what works best for you by experimenting with a variety of spells and techniques.

Words of power often rhyme so that they are easier to remember and resonate harmoniously. Memorization is not important, it is the intent of your words that matters. Your goal while casting a spell is to focus on the outcome, not the wording. If you will be distracted by trying to remember which words to say, then read them from your book of shadows or memorize them. If you are good at impromptu oration, just say what comes to mind.

Will all of my spells work?

Yes and no. All spells have some affect on you, but not every spell will manifest. Don't get frustrated, this happens to even the most experienced practitioners. Keep practicing and try casting at different times, moon phases, moods, etc. Perform divination to gain more insights about your situation and spell work.

I've been doing spells intuitively, without planning them according to moon phases or using specific candle colors. Are these things necessary for spells?

No, these things are not necessary. Using magical correspondences is an effective method to help you work with your power and natural energies but is not absolutely necessary for effective magic. Following your intuition will lead you to find what works best for you.

Should I cast spells for other people?

No. If your spell succeeds, you will hear knocks on your door twenty-four hours a day from those requesting your help. If the spell is not effective, you will be the scapegoat for every imaginable problem that occurs in the person's life. Failed spells can also lead to ridicule, which in turn drains your confidence and your ability to work successful magic in the future.

You must consider the ethical side of this situation. If you were to cast a spell for someone else, you would rob them of their chance to grow and develop. Self empowerment is what magic is all about. If this person doesn't know how to cast spells, teach them. If this person wants you do do a spell because they think spells are evil, then what does that say about who they think you are? It is best to direct them to prayer or mundane solutions in this last situation.

I made a mistake. How do I reverse a spell?

Imagine that you spent a great deal of time and energy planning on how to push a large boulder down a mountain. You implement this plan and the boulder is well on its way down the slope. Reversing or stopping this process is going to be tricky. Once set into motion, a spell can be difficult to break and often must simply run its course. To mitigate a spell's effects, use the Spell Reversal below or create your own and perform it during the waning moon. Also, be sure to disassemble any spell bags or bottles used for the original spell.

Spell Reversal

If you have any remaining ingredients from the original spell, such as sigils, botanicals, or bits of candle, collect them in a bowl. Anoint a white candle with rosemary essential oil, uncrossing oil, or olive oil and place it before you.

Allow yourself to relax and enter your magical mind state. Consider your motives for casting the original spell and reflect on how you might approach similar situations differently. Light the candle and visualize the spell you cast dissolving and unraveling. Use any words of power that you prefer or say:

Unravel, unbind, release and disperse,
I undo my spell that twisted to curse.
The energy focused is now free,
it will not harm nor turn on me.

If you collected ingredients in a bowl, pour water over them and sprinkle them with three pinches of salt. You may repeat the words of power as you do this.

Water tends to disperse spells, and salt is a classic purification tool. The combination of water and salt will wash out the original spell's power. You can burn the ingredients from the original spell, but some things emit toxins when they combust. Burning the items may send out the remaining energy from the original spell rather than dispersing it.

Allow the candle to burn down completely and dispose of everything. The easiest way to do this is to strain the water off into the sink and put everything in the trash. Empty the garbage, so it isn't inside your home by taking it to the dumpster or outdoor trash can.

How long will it take my spell to work?

Time can be tricky because magic is not necessarily bound by time and space. Certain spells have times specified in the actual wording such as "money will come, before this day is done". Including this type of time specification can *sometimes* be helpful. If a spell has not been successful within a full cycle of the moon, review your intentions, perform divination, make sure you've followed-up on the physical plane (jobs don't often appear when you don't apply), and try designing a new spell with a different approach.

I live with someone who wouldn't approve of me doing magic. Are there any discrete spells that don't require candles, incense or other occult-like tools?

You don't need tools to cast spells. Traditional tools will assist in focusing your intent but are certainly not necessary. If you are having difficulty focusing your energy and feel that tools will help, try to substitute more mundane appearing items such as flowers for the incense or colored light bulbs for candles. You can design your own spells that do not use occult-like tools.

What do I do with used spell ingredients?

Use common sense with your disposal and re-use everything you can. Do not throw spell ingredients into bodies of water. There are many environmental concerns regarding this, and it is wasteful and irresponsible.

Botanicals can be composted or broadcast onto the ground for the earth to reclaim. Spent candles can be thrown away, but I prefer to collect bits of candles until I have enough to melt down and make a new candle. When you burned the candle during the spell you released the energy and there is no sense in wasting the wax that is left. Cleanse your stones and crystals. There is no magical energy charge that cannot be cleansed from a stone that has been around millions of years before humans.

Spell bottles and bags can be dis-assembled and their items reused. Some spell bottles and bags are intended to stay around for a long period of time and can be buried in your yard (if they do not contain toxic ingredients) or tucked away in a protected area of your home.

Correspondences

This reference section will help you find just the right timing and ingredients for your spells. The correspondence tables use the following symbols to allow you to quickly find what you are looking for.

☂   Protection & Warding

❤   Love, Lust, Friendship

$ Money & Prosperity

♣   Luck & Good Fortune

⚡   Cleansing, Purification & Banishing

☽   Dream, Visions, Astral Travel & Divination

⚕   Health, Healing, Peace, Harmony

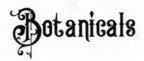

Botanicals

Check the oils list for additional botanicals such as anise and angelica. The properties of a natural essential oil are usually the same as for the plant material.

Botanical	☂	♥	$	♣	⚡	☾	⚕
Acorn	✔			✔			✔
Allspice		✔	✔	✔			✔
Almond		✔	✔			✔	
Aloe	✔			✔	✔		✔
Apple	✔	✔		✔			✔
Basil	✔	✔	✔		✔		
Bay	✔				✔	✔	✔
Benzoin	✔	✔	✔	✔	✔	✔	✔
Black Pepper	✔				✔		
Blackberry	✔		✔				✔
Cabbage		✔		✔			✔
Catnip	✔		✔	✔			✔
Cedar	✔	✔	✔	✔	✔	✔	✔
Chamomile	✔	✔	✔		✔	✔	✔
Chili & Cayenne		✔			✔		✔
Cinnamon	✔	✔	✔		✔		
Clove	✔	✔	✔		✔		✔
Copal	✔			✔	✔	✔	✔
Damiana		✔				✔	
Dandelion	✔		✔	✔		✔	✔

Botanicals

Botanical	☂	♥	$	♣	⚡	☽	⚕
Dragon's Blood	✓	✓	✓	✓	✓	✓	✓
Frankincense	✓			✓	✓	✓	✓
Garlic	✓				✓		✓
Ginger	✓	✓	✓				✓
Hibiscus		✓				✓	
Jasmine		✓	✓			✓	
Juniper	✓	✓	✓	✓	✓	✓	✓
Lavender	✓	✓			✓	✓	✓
Lemon		✓			✓		✓
Marigold (Calendula)	✓				✓	✓	✓
Marjoram	✓	✓	✓				✓
Mint		✓	✓	✓	✓		✓
Mugwort	✓				✓	✓	
Myrrh	✓		✓	✓	✓	✓	✓
Oak & Acorns	✓		✓	✓			✓
Orange		✓	✓	✓		✓	
Patchouli	✓	✓	✓				
Pine	✓		✓	✓	✓		✓
Raspberry	✓	✓					✓
Rose	✓	✓		✓		✓	✓
Rosemary	✓	✓			✓	✓	✓
Sage	✓				✓	✓	✓
Sandalwood	✓				✓	✓	✓
Strawberry		✓	✓	✓			
Sunflower	✓		✓				✓

Botanical	☂	❤	$	♣	⚡	☽	⚕
Thyme		✓			✓	✓	✓
Turmeric	✓				✓		✓
Vanilla		✓	✓				
Violet	✓	✓	✓	✓			✓
Willow	✓	✓				✓	✓
Wormwood	✓	✓			✓	✓	
Yarrow		✓			✓	✓	

Incense

All incense corresponds to both fire and air. You can use it to represent either element in a spell. Certain ingredients have an additional elemental emphasis. When a maker discloses some of the ingredients, you can extrapolate the magical use of the formula.

Let's use Soyeido's *Moss Garden* incense as an example. The package says it contains sandalwood, benzoin, patchouli, and spices. The aroma is delicate, woodsy, sweet, with a whisper of spice and slightly balsamic. You might associate this incense with earth (and the name certainly confirms this).

For incense not listed here, look up the incense ingredients or fragrance descriptions and refer to the correspondence tables for botanicals and oils.

Incense	☂	❤	$	♣	⚡	☽	⚕
Aastha (Satya)		✓	✓		✓	✓	
Aloeswood	✓		✓	✓	✓	✓	✓
Amber	✓	✓	✓	✓	✓	✓	
Bay Laurus nobilis	✓		✓		✓	✓	✓
Benzoin	✓	✓	✓	✓	✓		
Cedar	✓	✓	✓	✓	✓	✓	✓

Incense	☂	♥	$	♣	ϟ	☽	⚕
Cinnamon	✔	✔	✔		✔		
Citronella	✔	✔	✔				
Coconut		✔				✔	
Copal	✔			✔	✔	✔	✔
Dragon's Blood	✔	✔	✔	✔	✔		✔
Frankincense	✔			✔	✔	✔	✔
Honey		✔	✔	✔			✔
Sandalwood	✔	✔	✔	✔	✔	✔	✔
Musk		✔		✔			
Myrrh	✔			✔	✔	✔	✔
Nag Champa	✔	✔	✔	✔	✔	✔	✔
Opium		✔				✔	
Opopanax (Sweet Myrrh)	✔	✔	✔	✔	✔	✔	✔
Palo Santo	✔	✔	✔	✔	✔	✔	✔
Jasmine		✔	✔			✔	
Patchouli	✔	✔	✔				
Pine	✔		✔	✔	✔		✔
Rose	✔	✔		✔		✔	✔
Lavender	✔	✔			✔	✔	✔
Sage	✔				✔	✔	✔
Sandalwood	✔				✔	✔	✔
Strawberry		✔	✔	✔			
Styrax	✔	✔	✔	✔	✔		
Vanilla		✔	✔				

Oils

E after a name indicates a pure essential oil. These are steam distilled from the plant and frequently match the magical properties of the botanical. I've included the most affordable and easily obtainable essential oils for this chart. Check the botanicals list for additional oils. The properties of a natural essential oil are generally the same as for the plant material.

M after a name indicates a popular magical oil. The ingredients in these magical oils will vary depending on the creator however, the traditional uses remain the same.

Oil	☂	❤	$	♣	⚡	☽	⚕
Abramelin M	✓	✓	✓	✓	✓	✓	✓
Adam & Eve M		✓					
Angelica E	✓			✓	✓	✓	✓
Anise E	✓	✓	✓	✓	✓	✓	
Basil E	✓	✓	✓		✓		
Balsam Fir E	✓				✓	✓	✓
Bay E Laurus nobilis	✓		✓		✓	✓	✓
Bergamot E	✓		✓	✓		✓	✓
Black Cat M	✓			✓	✓	✓	
Cedar* E	✓	✓	✓	✓	✓	✓	✓
Chamomile E	✓	✓	✓		✓	✓	✓
Cinnamon E	✓	✓	✓	✓	✓		
Come to Me M		✓	✓	✓			
Dragon's Blood M	✓	✓	✓	✓	✓	✓	✓
Eucalyptus E	✓		✓		✓		✓

Oils

Oil	☂	❤	$	♣	⚡	☾	⚕
Florida Water M Oils in Alcohol	✔		✔	✔	✔	✔	
High John M	✔		✔	✔	✔		
Hot Foot M					✔		
Hoyt's Cologne Oils in Alcohol			✔	✔	✔		
Fast Luck M		✔	✔	✔			
Kananga Water M	✔	✔			✔	✔	
Four Thieves M	✔				✔		✔
Jezebel M		✔	✔				
Lavender E	✔	✔	✔	✔	✔	✔	✔
Lemon E	✔	✔			✔		✔
Lemongrass E	✔	✔	✔		✔	✔	✔
Orange E		✔	✔	✔		✔	
Peppermint E	✔	✔	✔	✔	✔	✔	✔
Road Opener M		✔	✔	✔	✔		
Rosemary	✔	✔	✔	✔	✔	✔	✔
Tea Tree	✔						✔
Uncrossing M	✔			✔	✔		
Van Van M	✔		✔	✔	✔		

* Cedar, cedarwood, altlas cedar, and Himalayan cedar all have the same correspondences.

Working With Moon Phases

There are many approaches to working with the phases of the moon. This four-phase approach is easy to remember and flows naturally with the primary energies of the phases. If your technique is different than this, don't worry! You can use any approach that you feel is right for you.

New: Start new projects and spells for growth, manifestation, or new beginnings. This is also a good time for cleansing, clearing, and protection.
Keywords: Resting, releasing, banishing, repelling, reversal magic, unbinding, new beginnings.
When: New moon energy lasts for three days - the day before the new moon, the day of, and the day after.

Waxing: This phase is excellent for attraction, drawing, growth, and spells to bring what you desire into your life. Your intentions grown and manifest as the moon waxes.
Keywords: Attraction, setting intentions, manifesting, planning, planting, developing, drawing, attraction.
When: From two days after the new moon to two days before the full moon.

Full: This is a great time for any type of magic or divination, and is a time of celebration and gratitude.
Keywords: Celebration, harvest, gratitude, meditation, devotion, protection, magical power.
When: Full moon energy lasts for three days - the day before the full moon, the day of, and the day after.

Waning: This is a time of cleansing and releasing intentions that were not meant to manifest. Work on spells for reducing and banishing.
Keywords: Clearing, cleansing, releasing, reversals, re-evaluation, banishing.
When: From two days after the full moon to two days before the new moon.

Magical Days of the Week

Monday: New beginnings, balancing emotions, intuition, shadow work, dreams, psychic abilities. Planet: Moon

Tuesday: Legal matters, courage, confidence, action, justice, protection, reversal, passion, banishing. Planet: Mars

Wednesday: Reflection, devotion, divination, travel, luck, communication, knowledge, healing. Planet: Mercury

Thursday: Money, prosperity, cleansing, marriage, luck, growth, oaths, success, influence. Planet: Jupiter

Friday: Love, romance, passion, beauty, home, family, fertility, art, sexuality, birth and rebirth. Planet: Venus

Saturday: Banishing, cleansing, meditation, protection, transformation, binding, spirit/ancestor contact. Planet: Saturn

Sunday: Success, growth, protection, inspiration, defense, strength, power, healing. Planet: Sun

Color Correspondences

Red: Lust, passion, sex, vigor, magnetism, virility, energy, love.

Pink: Unconditional love, beauty, emotional love, friendship.

Orange: Courage, potency, invigoration, stimulation, stamina.

Yellow: Happiness, mental stimulation, warmth, attraction.

Green: Fertility, growth, luck, balance, harmony, prosperity.

Light Blue: Healing, peace, spirituality, communication.

Dark Blue & Indigo: Psychic skills, intuition, wisdom.

Purple & Violet: Connection to the divine, spirituality, royalty, expansion, magical energy, influencing others, psychic skills.

Black: Absorbing, banishing, reversals, protection, grounding.

Gray: Protection, shielding, dreams, meditation, neutralizing.

White: Protection, peace, purity, meditation, divine connection.

Brown: Earth energy, animals and familiars, grounding.

Silver: The moon, feminine principle, clairvoyance, magic.

Gold: The sun, masculine principle, wealth, growth, abundance

Moon Sign Magic

Moon Sign	Conducive and favorable to these types of magic.
♈ Aries	Confidence, New Projects, Energy, Motivation, Justice, Protection, Success, Breakthroughs, Progress
♉ Taurus	Creativity, Sensuality, Romance, Security, Money, Prosperity, Grounding, Property, Gratitude, Growth
♊ Gemini	Relationships, Balance, Harmony, Communication, Mental Powers, Attraction
♋ Cancer	Love, Relationships, Fertility, Family, Creativity, Nurturing, Intuition, Psychic Skills, Divination, Home
♌ Leo	Friendship, Love, Romance, Optimism, Passion, Creativity, Strength, Charisma
♍ Virgo	Purification, Waning, Banishing, Healing, Writing, Organizing, Grounding, Exorcism
♎ Libra	Balance, Beauty, Connecting, Justice, Legal Matters, Marriage, Creativity, Revealing Truth, Partnerships
♏ Scorpio	Exploring Your Shadows, Personal Growth, Change, Sensuality, Passion, Psychic Skills, Divination, Releasing, Protection
♐ Sagittarius	Confidence, Luck, Planning, Divination, Adventure, Fun, Travel, Gambling, Revealing Truth, Career Success
♑ Capricorn	Releasing, Banishing, Productivity, Focus, Bond-Breaking, Reversals, Self-Promotion
♒ Aquarius	Expression, Friendship, Psychic Skills, Meditation, Releasing Habitual Thought Patterns
♓ Pisces	Spirit and Ancestral Contact, Intuition, Divination, Healing, Meditations, Shielding, Obfuscating, Psychic Skills

Earth

Astrological Signs: Taurus, Virgo, Capricorn	
Colors: Green and Brown	Direction: North
Ritual Tools: Pentacle	Tarot Suit: Pentacles
Botanicals: Alfalfa, Barley, Beet, Buckwheat, Comfrey, Corn, Cotton, Cypress, Fern, Grains, Honesty, Honeysuckle, Horehound, Horsetail, Knotweed, Mugwort, Oats, Patchouli, Potato, Primrose, Rhubarb, Rye, Sage, Tulip, Turnip, Vervain, Vetivert, Wheat, Wood Sorrel	
Stones: Black Tourmaline, Calcite, Emerald, Green and Brown Jasper, Hematite, Jade, Jet, Malachite, Moss Agate, Onyx, Peridot, Tree Agate	

Air

Astrological Signs: Gemini, Libra, Aquarius	
Colors: Yellow	Direction: East
Ritual Tools: Wand or Athame	Tarot Suit: Swords
Botanicals: Agrimony, Almond, Anise, Bean, Benzoin, Bergamot, Bittersweet, Borage, Broom, Caraway, Chicory, Dandelion, Endive, Goldenrod, Hazel, Lavender, Lemongrass, Lemon verbena, Lily of the valley, Mace, Marjoram, Meadowsweet, Mint, Mistletoe, Mulberry, Parsley, Pine, Pistachio, Rice, Sage, Senna, Slippery elm, Star anise	
Stones: Aventurine, Citrine, Clear Quartz, Mica, Opal, Smokey Quartz, Tiger's Eye, Topaz, Turquoise	

 Fire

Astrological Signs: Aries, Leo, Sagittarius	
Colors: Red, Orange	Direction: South
Ritual Tools: Athame or Wand	Tarot Suit: Wands

Botanicals: Allspice, Angelica, Basil, Bay, Cactus, Carnation, Cedar, Chili Pepper, Chrysanthemum, Cinnamon, Clove, Copal, Coriander, Cumin, Damiana, Dragon's Blood, Fennel, Frankincense, Galangal, Garlic, Ginger, Ginseng, Goldenseal, Hawthorn, High John the Conqueror, Holly, Hyssop, Marigold, Mullein, Mustard, Nutmeg, Onion, Orange, Pennyroyal, Pepper, Peppermint, Pomegranate, Rosemary, Rue, Saffron, St John's Wort, Sesame, Sunflower, Thistle, Witch hazel, Wormwood, Yucca

Stones: Amber, Carnelian, Clear Quartz, Fire Agate, Fire Opal, Lava Stone, Red Jasper, Sunstone

 Water

Astrological Signs: Cancer, Scorpio, Pisces	
Colors: Blue	Direction: West
Ritual Tools: Cauldron or Cup	Tarot Suit: Cups

Botanicals: Aloe, Apple, Apricot, Blackberry, Burdock, Camellia, Cardamom, Catnip, Chickweed, Coconut, Comfrey, Daffodil, Daisy, Elder, Elm, Eucalyptus, Feverfew, Foxglove, Gardenia, Grape, Hibiscus, Hyacinth, Iris, Jasmine, Larkspur, Lemon, Lilac, Lily, Lotus, Mimosa, Morning Glory, Myrrh, Myrtle, Orchid, Orris Root, Pansy, Passion Flower, Pear, Periwinkle, Plum, Poppy, Rose, Spearmint, Spikenard, Strawberry, Sugar Cane, Sweet Pea, Tansy, Thyme, Valerian, Violet, Willow, Wintergreen, Yarrow

Stones: Amethyst, Aquamarine, Azurite, Blue Topaz, Celestite, Chrysocolla, Coral, Lapis Lazuli, Moonstone, Pearl, Sapphire, Selenite, Sodalite

Stones & Crystals

These gifts from the earth are extremely useful tools for magic and meditation. They add powerful energy and can be cleansed and re-used indefinitely.

Stones are difficult to categorize into the various uses such as love, money, healing, etc. because their uses will be specific to how they resonate with you. As you work with an individual specimen, it may reveal additional uses. A good way to get started is to to use the color of the stones as a general indication of their purposes.

For example, if you wish to stimulate your psychic skills, you might try a stone that is blue or purple. Lapis lazuli and sodalite are both blue and are used to enhance psychic skills and communication. These might be good choices if you are doing tarot readings for other people so you can tap into your insight and find the words to express what you discover. Purple amethyst or fluorite would also be good choices for stimulating psychic and mental powers.

Once you've narrowed down your choices, hold each stone or place it near you and relax as if you are preparing yourself for casting a spell. Notice how the energy of the stone makes you feel. Are there certain thoughts, feelings, or memories that enter your mind? Do you have any physical reactions such as tingling, shivers, goosebumps, pressure, temperature changes, etc. Choose the stone or combination of stones that evoke the energy in you that will align with your goals.

Amazonite
A type of feldspar. Harmony, blending many energies, peace, calm, communication.

Amber
Amber is one of the earliest stones used by humans in religion and magic. It is a traditional amulet worn by witches and is often combined with jet. It is considered a gemstone, but is not a mineral. Amber is the fossilized resin of ancient trees, and its use dates back to the Neolithic period. Power, purification, protection from negativity, shielding, protection from psychic and magical vampirism, healing, power, energy, sun energy.

Amethyst
Enhances general magical workings, raises personal power, psychic development, protection, detoxification, inner exploration, emotional and psychic shielding, purification, breaking addictions, self-understanding.

Apache Tears
A special variety of volcanic obsidian. Protection and shielding, emotional cleansing, grounding.

Black Tourmaline
Probably the best all-around protection stone. It tends to need less cleansing than many stones. Protection, purification, shielding, grounding, neutralizing, detoxification, prevents psychic and magical drain, anti-hex, converts negative energy into neutral energy.

Bloodstone
A red and green chalcedony. Strength, healing, courage, detoxification, purification, balancing, energizing, grounding of sexual and emotional centers, physical healing.

Botswana Agate
This stone both soothes and energizes. Clearing conflict, harmony, absorbs negativity, prevents unwanted visitors, breaking bonds, anti-hex, breaking old patterns or addictions, prevents obsessing.

Carnelian
Focus, confidence, motivation, willpower, concentration, uplifting, energizing, protection, sexuality, prevents emotional and psychic vampirism, reinforces the aura.

Celestite
Connection with divine, facing fears, dreams, visions, healing.

Citrine
Energy, enlightenment, manifestation, creativity, uplifting, happiness, inner strength, protection.

Clear Quartz
A very useful stone for any magical purpose. Power, protection, harmony, energy, healing, focus, clarity, willpower, purification.

Fluorite
The color of individual specimens often indicates their uses, ranging from green (healing) to purple (psychic work) and more. This stone activates the mind, including mental and psychic powers. It can help open the doors of perception and improve mental clarity for decision making, divination or study. Cleansing, purifying, healing, psychic enhancement.

Stones & Crystals

Garnet
Healing broken hearts, physical health, strength, sexual expression, self-worth, attraction, lust, protection, fertility.

Green Aventurine
Increases opportunities and your ability to perceive opportunities, confidence, growth, personal energy, vitality, perception, prosperity, luck, attraction, love.

Hawk's Eye
This is a type of tiger's eye stone in blue, green and gray colors. Clarity, truth, gaining perspective, psychic powers, visions, psychic protection, divination, magical power, perceiving opportunities, stamina.

Hematite
Manifestation, potency, charisma, grounding, balancing of opposites, detoxification, strength, courage, virility, confidence.

Jasper
See Mookaite Jasper, Picture Jasper, Red Jasper.

Jet
Like amber, jet is a potent amulet used since ancient times. This is one of the earliest stones used by humans and is a traditional witch's amulet. Although jet is a gemstone it is a mineraloid, not a mineral. It comes from the wood from ancient coniferous trees that has been transformed over millions of years under extreme pressure. Protection, purification, manifesting, stress relief, grief support, dispelling negative patterns, grounding, connecting to earth and moon energies. Witches traditionally combine jet with amber.

Kyanite
Clarity, purification, protection, power, telepathy, intuition, communication, balance, dream work, meditation.

Lapis Lazuli
Creativity, visualization, expression, articulation, communication, intuition, divination, psychic powers, visualizing, manifesting.

Mahogany Obsidian
Strength, healing, confidence, breaking bonds, stability, grounding, unblocking, protection.

Malachite
Analyzing internal patterns, memory, healing, balance, confidence, business and money acumen.

Mookaite Jasper
Earth energy, increasing awareness, identifying truth.

Moonstone
Self-acceptance, confidence, intuition, psychic powers, moon and Goddess energy, balance, calm, dreams, truth, helps identify and

work with cycles and patterns, intuition, inspiration, creativity.

Picture Jasper
Earth energy, harmony, gaining perspective, insight, manifestation, visualization, nurturing, confidence.

Red Jasper
Balancing, handling emotional stress, dreams, strength, stability, grounding, healing.

Red Tiger's Eye & Golden Cat's Eye
The red form is tiger's eye and the yellow form is cat's eye. Both are useful for protection, perception, clear thinking, discovering the truth, luck, opportunities, willpower, grounding, vitality, balance, insight, motivation, integrity, stamina, clarity.

Rhodonite
Stabilize emotions, grounding, revealing hidden talents, compassion, love, understanding.

Rose Quartz
Heals emotions, self-love, self-acceptance, forgiveness, happiness, calming, unconditional love, beauty, creativity, receptivity, peace, friendship.

Ruby
Vitality, courage, confidence, sensuality, passion, sexuality, attraction, energy, motivation, aspiration, confidence.

Sapphire
Balance, healing, calm, awareness, power, faithfulness, fidelity, psychic skills, communication.

Selenite
Cleansing, purification, awareness, psychic skills, insight, harmony, clarity, peace.

Shiva Lingham
Meditation, insight, healing, balance, energy, psychic skills, union of opposites, wisdom, sexual healing, virility.

Smokey Quartz
Protection, grounding, shielding.

Snowflake Obsidian
Grounding, centering, protection, revealing what is hidden, healing, psychic awareness, returning lost objects, intuition.

Sodalite
Inspirations creativity, mental powers, communication, creativity, teaching, psychic shielding, logic.

Tiger Iron
Tiger iron combines the energies of red jasper, tiger eye, and hematite. Manifestation, protection, energy, strength, stamina, willpower, motivation, healing, grounding, creativity.

Tourmalated Quartz
Shielding, protection, anti-hex, purification, cleansing, neutral-izes baneful energy, power, balance, grounding, manifestation.
Tourmaline
See Black Tourmaline
Unakite
Balance, emotional healing, peace, stability, release.
Watermelon Tourmaline
Balance, self-love, healing, attraction, protection.
Wavellite
Earth energy, manifestation, insight, understanding connections, healing, finding your path, optimism.
Zebra Stone
Insight, grounding, manifesting, love, harmony, happiness, creativity, protection.

Your Correspondences

Use this worksheet to expand your correspondences for the items you have on hand or that aren't listed in your almanac. Perhaps your favorite incense has a special association for you, or your correspondences for some ingredients are different than the traditional ones.

Item	☂	♥	$	♣	ϟ	☾	⚕

Record Keeping

Use the templates in this section to inspire you. These templates give you an idea of what types of information to include in your book of shadows. You may wish to help keep your writing private by using a magical alphabet or substitution cipher for key points such as the names of individuals.

Theban Script

Theban script is a substitution cipher that is easy to use and read with a little practice.

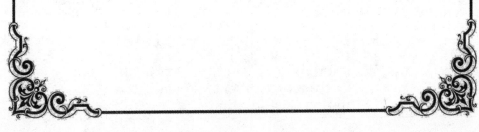

Divination Spreads

Divination spreads or layouts can be used with tarot cards, oracle cards, runes, and other forms of divination in which you cast lots. Spreads are a way in which you arrange or "lay out" your divination tools to give you a better understanding of their meaning to you. Before you begin a divination session decide which layout you will use and what the positions will mean to you. It is highly recommended that you perform divination prior to casting a spell. Record all your readings in your book of shadows or divination journal. An example of a divination record is included on the next page.

Three Position Spreads

☆	☆	☆
Current Situation	Probable Outcome	Suggested Action

☆	☆	☆
Past	Present	Future

☆	☆	☆
You	The Relationship	Your Partner(s)

Six Position Spread

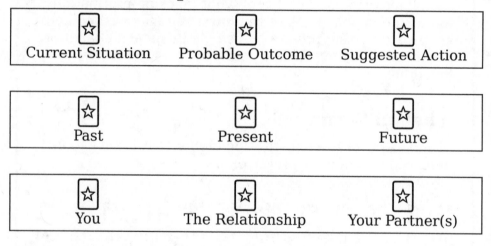
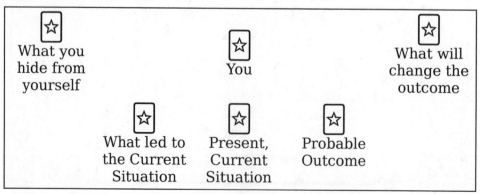

What you hide from yourself

You

What will change the outcome

What led to the Current Situation

Present, Current Situation

Probable Outcome

Divination Record

It is a good idea to record any daily divination sessions, periodic readings, or pre-spell consultations. Record keeping will help you become more proficient in your divination skills. This worksheet can be used with tarot cards, oracle cards, runes, or other forms of divination where you draw or cast lots. Lay out your tools in whichever spread you have chosen. Consider the questions below and record your reading.

Date	Time	Moon Phase	My Mood
August 1, 2023	*8:30 pm*	*Super Full Moon*	*Anxious*

Tool Used	Subject, Question, or Situation
Rider-Waite Tarot Deck	*Should I take the job offer?*

Record the specific cards or runes drawn and their positions.

5 of Pentacles	*6 of Wands*	*Ace of Pentacles*
Current Situation	*Probable Outcome*	*Suggested Action*

What is the first thing I noticed?

The couple in the 5 of pentacles show how I feel, broke and left out.

Are there numbers, colors, or symbols that repeat throughout the spread? Do these have special meaning to me?

I expected pentacles because my question is about work. I didn't expect the outcome to be one of victory, and accomplishment.

My feelings and impressions about the reading.
I am confident that this job change is for the best.
My anxiety is a little bit less.

My Interpretation
Current: I feel isolated at work and do not make enough money.
Probable Outcome: Success and more confidence and recognition.
Suggested Action: Take the new job!

Follow-up (Insights gained after a month.)
I can't believe how much easier life has been since I took the new job. My stress levels are lower and I've made some friends at work. I only make a little more than my last job, but there are reviews and raises every six months. I'm also doing less 'retail therapy' so I'm spending a lot less.

𝒟aily 𝒟raw

Drawing a card or rune every day is a good way to improve your divination skills.

Date	Time	Moon Phase	My Mood
May 22, 2023	8:00 am	Waxing	Not awake yet

Card or Rune	What colors, symbols, or numbers stand out in the card? For runes, what comes to mind first?
Chariot	Blue stars above the figure.

My Interpretation
I feel like this is a message for me to take the reigns and be driven toward my guiding star.

Evening or Next Morning Follow-up
I was driven and stayed on task all day, but my co-worker also offered to sell me their car. It is a really good deal. Maybe this card referred to both my drive, and a literal chariot!

𝒟ream 𝒟ecord

Recording dreams is an interesting way to gain insight into your mind or help you recognize any precognitive dreams. Record your dreams soon after waking for the best recall of details. Because our linear minds are not yet fully awake, a simple template is best. Begin recording the dream and as you become fully awake fill in the time and date information.

Date	Time	Moon Phase
December 5, 2023	4:00 am	Waning

What I Recall
I was in a canoe with my partner and they fell overboard.
I grabbed their hand to help them back into the canoe and they turned into an anchor.

My Interpretation
I have been feeling like my partner has been dragging me down and this was probably my subconscious illustrating that.

Spell Record

Purpose of Spell (My Goal)
Happiness Spell

Pre-spell divination

⭐	⭐	⭐
Present	**Spell Advice**	**Outcome of Spell**
9 of Swords	*Magician*	*6 of Wands*

My interpretation

I've had a lot of anxiety lately as is clear with the 9 of Swords. The Magician suggests that I can manifest the change I seek. The outcome indicates victory.

Date & Time	Moon Phase	My Mood
Sept. 29, 2023 *7:30 am*	*Full Moon*	*Stressed and anxious but confident my spell will help.*

Correspondence Notes
Color: Yellow
Oils: Helichrysum and Lavender
Stones: Rose Quartz
Herbs: Catnip

I prepared anointing oil for the candle: 3 drops each helichrysum essential oil and lavender essential oil in 5 mL jojoba oil.

Anointed a yellow candle. Placed it in the center of the altar and sprinkled catnip around it in a circle. Focused on the things I have to be grateful for while holding the rose quartz. Continued focusing on gratitude while saying my words of power -
I release my anxieties and fears
I can work through any challenges
I have many blessings in my life
and I know there are many more to come.
Allowed candle to burn down and kept the rose quartz near my bed.

Follow-up
It has been a month and I've felt much more optimistic.

Articles

Pick up a new skill with the instructions for reading tea leaves, or get some food for thought with these articles.

How to Read Tea Leaves

The art of divination by tea leaves is known as tasseomancy. Tea leaf reading was popular in the 1920s and is currently experiencing a revival. Reading tea leaves for yourself and others can be fun and entertaining as well as insightful. It allows you to explore and develop your psychic skills and your conversation skills. Sharing a cup of tea and conversation can be a delight that is enhanced with a little wisdom about reading the leaves.

What Type of Tea to Use

It is best to use a loose tea with a medium to long leaf. You can use tea from teabags or even coffee grounds but it is easier to discern shapes and symbols with long leaves. You can also use green tea such as "gunpowder" or "jasmine pearls." Both of these are long leaves which are tightly rolled into small balls that unfurl in your cup. A good "English breakfast" found in tins at your grocer will also work well.

Flavored teas can open up interesting possibilities. You can pair your tea with flavors that suit your purpose. Jasmine is great for readings about relationships and love. Earl gray will help with contemplation for any situation. Mint is excellent for matters of money and business. For other flavors, check the magical correspondences of different herbs.

193

How to Prepare the Cup

Prepare a cup for everyone present. It is important to share in the tea drinking even if you are only reading the leaves for someone else. This gives you the full experience and helps connect you with others present. Set up your area with comfortable seating, napkins, sweeteners, cream, cookies or biscuits, and perhaps a candle. Create an atmosphere that will help you relax. Light some candles and fire up the aromatherapy diffuser or burn some incense.

- Place ½ to 1 teaspoon of tea into the bottom of each teacup. You'll want to use a little less tea than you normally would for each cup.
- Pour freshly boiled water over the tea in the cup.
- Sit comfortably and chat. If you are alone, clear your mind and relax. You might pull a few tarot or oracle cards while you wait for the tea to steep. You may stir your tea after a minute to help submerge any floating leaves.
- As soon as the tea is cool enough to drink, begin sipping. When there is less than a tablespoon of liquid left in the cup, gently swirl the cup, allow it to settle a bit, and tip it upside down on top of the saucer. You don't have to do this for your own cup if you are only reading for someone else. It is normal for some leaves to spill out onto the saucer. If no leaves remain in the cup, try again and sip more of the liquid before tipping your cup over. Some readers regard the leaves left in the saucer as representing what you've left behind (the querent's past).
- Gently turn the cup upright and hold it front of you.

See and Interpret Symbols

Gaze into the cup and allow your mind to form images in the patterns of the leaves. Take a few deep breaths and let your intuition flow. Expand your imagination and try to shift the focus of your eyes from blurry to sharp. If you ever tried to discern shapes in clouds, tea leaf reading is similar. Your intuition will guide your imagination to see the shapes that mean the most to your subconscious.

Use the traditional interpretations that start on the next page to help understand the meanings of the shapes you discern. Traditional meanings are a good place to start but always allow your intuition and instincts to take precedence. If an axe has negative associations for you, seeing it in the cup might not mean 'victory' as is traditionally thought. Listen to your gut.

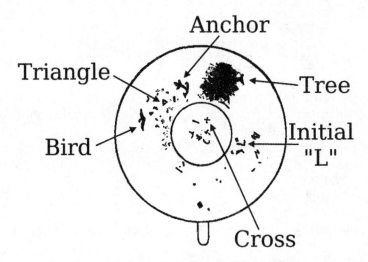

One might interpret the cup above as follows: the bird and triangle indicate good news. If that news is from a lover, the anchor indicates that this relationship is stable. The large tree indicates money and happiness. A message will be received by someone with the initial "L", and the cross may indicate a need for protection in the distant future.

Timing What You See

The location of the symbols in the cup will indicate time or meaning. There are special tea leaf reading cups that are divided into time periods or astrological houses. These are not necessary as the easiest method is to use top-down timing.

Symbols appearing near the top of the cup are in the present, those in the middle are the near future such as within a month. Symbols at the bottom of the cup are the outcome or distant future. There are many variations to cup divisions and time periods. As you come across new methods try them out to see if they resonate with you. Whatever method you choose, decide which one you will use before you begin each reading.

Tasseomancy Symbols

Acorn health, affection, strength
Aircraft unsuccessful or failed projects. Aircraft can be balloons, planes, or anything related
Anchor luck, success in business, stable relationship
Angel good news
Apes secret enemies
Apples long life, success
Arch a journey abroad
Arrow disappointing news from the direction the arrow points
Axe victory
Badger long life and prosperity as a single (unmarried)
Basket an addition to the family
Bat fruitless journeys or tasks
Bear a long period of travel
Birds a lucky sign; good travel
Boat company coming
Bouquet luck with friends, love life, and money
Bridge a good journey
Building stability, new property
Bull slander by an enemy
Butterfly success and pleasure
Camel patience and endurance
Candle enlightenment, study, strength in dark times
Cannon good fortune
Car or Truck wealth approaching
Cart fluctuations of fortune, labor pays off
Castle unexpected fortune, inheritance, or a legacy
Cat good luck, trust intuition and gut instincts, comfort
Church or Cathedral great prosperity, spiritual connection
Cattle prosperity
Chain an early marriage; if broken, trouble lies ahead
Chair an addition to the family
Circles money or gifts
Clouds trouble brewing on the horizon, fertile field
Clover luck, happiness, prosperity
Cock prosperity
Coffin long sickness or sign of death of a near
Comet misfortune and trouble
Compass travel, finding your path, finding home
Cross trouble, delay, need for protection
Crow or Raven a message to pay attention, be aware

Crown success, honor, prestige
Deer disputes, failure in trade
Dog luck, faithful friends, money
Donkey a legacy long awaited
Dove luck, prosperity
Dragon big and sudden changes
Duck business success
Eagle relocation brings success
Elephant luck, health
Falcon a persistent enemy
Ferret active enemies
Fish good news from abroad
Flag danger from wounds inflicted by an enemy
Fox backstabbing, gossip, treachery by a trusted friend
Frog or Toad success in love and business, new beginnings
Gallows good luck
Goat enemies around
Goose happiness, successful venture.
Grasshopper good fortune, a friend will become a soldier
Gun discord, disaster, slander
Hammer victory
Hand read in conjunction with nearby symbols, receiving
Harp marriage, success in love
Hat success in life
Hawk an enemy
Heart pleasures to come; $ if surrounded by dots, marriage if surrounded by a circle or ring
Hen money, new family member
Horse desires fulfilled
Horseshoe a lucky trip, good partner, good luck
Hourglass imminent peril
House success in business
Ivy honor and happiness through faithful friends
Jackal a sly person who need not be feared
Jockey successful speculation, good odds
Jug or Bottle good health
Key money, increasing trade, and a good partner, unlocking mysteries, Hecate, talents emerging
Kite a long trip leading to success
Knife need to maintain friendships
Ladder travel
Letters news, initials
Lines travel and direction of travel; wavy≈hard, straight=easy
Lion aid of powerful friends
Mermaid mysteries revealed, misfortune for the seafaring
Money or $ fortune coming

Tasseomancy Symbols

Monkey deception in love
Moon happiness, prosperity, money
Mountain powerful friends; many mountains=many enemies
Mouse danger of poverty through theft or overspending
Mushroom sudden separation of lovers after a fight
Oak very lucky, long life, good health, money, strength
Owl wisdom, insight, warning, need to watch carefully
Palm Tree good luck, success
Peacock success, money, fame
Peacock Feather conceit, vanity, overrated
Pear money, improved social status, good partnership
Pig faithful lover but envious friends
Pigeons important messages
Pine Tree happiness
Rabbit success in a city or large town, prosperity, fertility
Rat loss due to enemies or employees
Razor lovers' quarrels and separation
Rifle discord, destruction
Ring marriage; nearby letters may indicate spouse's initial
Rose luck, good fortune, secrets
Saw strangers bring trouble
Scales legal battles
Scissors fights, separation, illness
Serpent or Snakes be cautious, spiteful enemies, bad luck
Shark danger
Sheep success, prosperity
Ship a successful journey
Spider money coming
Squares comfort, stability, peace
Star luck; if surrounded by dots foretells wealth and prestige
Swallow a good journey
Swan happy relationships, luck

A star appears at the bottom-left.

Sword dispute, lovers' quarrels; a broken sword=victory
Trees luck, prosperity, happiness
Triangles luck, inheritance
Trident success
Umbrella trouble, need protection
Unicorn scandal, magic
Vulture bitter enemies
Wheel inheritance, change
Windmill business success
Wolf jealousy
Zebra travel

Moon Void of Course

Every lunar month the moon moves through the twelve zodiac signs as indicated in your almanac with notations such as ☽♐ for moon in Sagittarius. We use this information to work with moon sign energies in our magic.

As the moon moves through the current zodiac sign, there is a moment when it makes its last contact with any planet in that sign. From that moment until the moon enters the next sign, it is *void of course*. This period can last from a few minutes to a couple of days.

This year you'll find data for the moon void of course included in the planner pages for the first time in 25 years. This data is shown on the relevant days as ☽ V/C.

The noted astrologer Al H. Morrison promoted incorporating this information into astrological techniques. As astrology increases in popularity, there is more understanding of what V/C means, and demand for ☽ V/C information has increased.

When casting spells using moon signs, you may wish to avoid doing so during ☽ V/C because the energy of that moon sign is thought to be weaker or more diffuse. Some people feel that ☽ V/C causes difficulties in concentration and decision-making. They will often set aside these times for more passive activities such as meditation, yoga, divination, and devotion.

Critical Thinking & Objectivity

Many concepts in the magical world require you to maintain your objectivity and critical thinking. It is easy to head into dubious territory when we uphold beliefs without this scrutiny. Without critical thinking, Mercury retrograde can be blamed for every trouble, but sometimes a utility gets shut off because the bill didn't get paid. Holding onto someone who you were told is your twin flame or soul mate might be enabling a harmful relationship. There are people who are afraid of Friday the 13th even though it is considered especially auspicious to others.

Moon void of course is used as *just one factor* by professional astrologers, but it has been edging into the realm of superstition over the past two years. I encourage you to remain mindful while exploring these and other magical concepts. Believing that something is inauspicious can often cause it to be so.

Beware of Frauds

You will encounter people who offer to do psychic readings or cast spells for you, for a price! Even free services may come with a cost that is not immediately apparent. Anyone offering to do unsolicited readings or magic on your behalf is offering to take your power away from you. A legitimate reader that you have sought out should be appropriately compensated for their time and expertise. However, when it comes to magic and spells, only you should be doing magic for yourself.

No matter how inexperienced you are, you have the power to cast effective spells. Never pay someone else to take the realization of that power away from you.

Some people will prey on you in desperate times and offer to reunite you with a lost love or bring you riches and fame. These predators use your desperation and desires to make money. You may also come across megalomaniacal charlatans who call themselves mages, wizards, witches, warlocks, magicians, spiritual advisors, psychics, channelers, doctors of love, or what have you.

The first way to know that they are fakes is that they are offering to do a spell for you instead of giving you the knowledge to do one for yourself. The second way to know they are bogus is that they charge large amounts of money or want repeated payments.

These charlatans know human nature very well; it is their business! They may entrap you in their con game by saying they are more powerful than you because of their experience. This is not true. You have more power to change your life than anyone else. Other entrapments may include offering services for free but requiring you to send them spell ingredients such as gold and silver coins, expensive purses, or other valuable items. For example, they may insist that your engagement ring must be cleansed and they must perform an elaborate secret ritual without you present. Most likely, this ritual is held at their local pawn shop.

I've had numerous encounters with frauds and their victims. Many people confided in me and said they were swindled because a fraud told them they would be safe from evil. The con artist explained that spells are evil, so instead of involving you in such things, they will do it on your behalf. This is simply preposterous! Spells, like prayers, meditation, and mantras, are tools of focus and have nothing to do with evil. Your primary weapon against these people is knowledge!

These con artists are exceedingly insecure! If you use the tarot, you will often find that they appear as the Magician card in reverse. They lack control of their lives, so they are driven to control others. Their magical and psychic skills are usually quite nominal and are merely supplemented by an acute ability to manipulate and deceive. Because they lack real skills, they are drawn to and prey upon people with genuine talent.

Frequently, their knowledge of magic and spells is superficial. A few well-placed questions will usually expose them as frauds. Ask if they are Wiccan. They aren't well versed in magic if they don't know what that is or say it is devil worship. Ask what the spell they are using entails. If they explain that it is a secret or that it would be too complicated for you to understand, they are not interested in helping you empower yourself. Can you purchase just the spell instructions from them? If not, why? Does the reason they give resonate with the truth?

Listen to your heart. Do you feel positive, confident, and in control after you speak with this person? Do you feel they will do something harmful to you if you do not follow their advice? Do you believe that this person is your last resort? If you answered yes to any of these three questions, leave the con artist behind and never look back.

Understanding the cunning with which these charlatans work is essential so you do not get trapped in their snares. The only help that a con artist will give you is to lighten the weight of your bank account and provide you with something to blame. A skillful con artist will help you relinquish your fears by giving you a scapegoat for your troubles, such as bad luck or a curse. This "blame-game" service is the most they can provide, and while offering this service, they steal an excellent opportunity for you to empower yourself.

Take-Away

If someone asks you for money or valuables to work magic, they aren't empowering you and are probably fakes. Never pay someone else to take the realization of your power away from you. You can cast spells and do your own readings. When you want a second opinion, you can usually trade readings with others. Legitimate, professional readers will not solicit you for readings, and their prices are clearly stated up-front.

Recipes

No almanac would be complete without that traditional recipes section. Whether you practice kitchen witchery or ceremonial magic, these recipes will serve you well.

All of the herbs, spices, and resins used in these recipes should be dried. When a recipe calls for Base Oil, use a stable oil that won't go rancid quickly such as Sunflower, Jojoba, Meadowfoam, Castor, or Coconut.

Dragon's Blood Oil

Ingredients
- 1 tablespoon Dragon's Blood Resin, crushed or powdered
- 2 tablespoons Base Oil
- 6 drops Clove Bud essential oil
- 1 teaspoon Sandalwood essential oil
- 3 drops Vetiver essential oil

Dragon's blood resin is an energy amplifier. It adds power to any magical working and is especially useful for protection, purification, love, and lust.

You'll want to infuse your base oil with dragon's blood for a complete lunar cycle. On a full moon, combine the dragon's blood resin, base oil, and clove bud oil in a bottle. Shake it well and store it in a cool, dark place. Do not refrigerate.

Shake the bottle of oil at least twice a week. When the moon is full again, it is time to filter your oil. Shake it well and pour it through several layers of cheesecloth. You can use a fine coffee filter in a funnel for a very clear oil. Filtering your oil through a coffee filter may take some time. I use a pour-through coffee set-up and leave it to filter overnight.

Fill a bottle with your filtered oil and add the sandalwood and vetiver oil. You may add a small chunk of dragon's blood resin (not crushed or powdered) to the bottle if you wish.

Protection Oil

Ingredients
- 1 pinch Angelica Root
- 1 pinch Frankincense or 9 drops Frankincense essential oil
- 1 pinch Basil or 3 drops Basil essential oil
- 1 Black Tourmaline crystal
- 2 Tablespoons Base Oil

Select a bottle that will accommodate the tourmaline crystal. Fill the bottle with all of the ingredients and use as an anointing oil for candles and tools. You can use this oil on your body or add it to your bath water for personal protection.

Attraction Oil

Ingredients
- 1 pinch Cinnamon chips or 3 drops Cinnamon essential oil
- 9 drops Patchouli essential oil
- 1 pinch Mint or 1 drop Mint essential oil (peppermint or spearmint)
- 1 pinch of Whole Cloves or 3 drops Clove Bud essential oil
- 1 Tablespoon Base Oil
- Optional: Rose Quartz or Green Aventurine stones

This anointing oil is for general drawing and attraction. Make this oil during the waxing moon. You can use this oil to attract love, money, friends, etc. You don't need to focus on a specific intent as you make this oil. Instead, use it for any attraction and focus your intention when you put it to use.

This *mise en place* style of witchery is like setting up dominos so you can tip them into action when you are ready. You might use this oil to boost your chances at a job one day and later use it to help you attract friends.

If you prefer to refine the focus of this oil, you can add rose quartz to the bottle to emphasize love and friendship. For attracting luck and money use the prosperity variation below.

Prosperity Variation

Ingredients
- Attraction Oil (see above)
- Green Aventurine
- Shredded currency
- 1 pinch Basil or 1 drop Basil essential oil

The U.S. Federal Reserve distributes shredded currency as a novelty souvenir. This unique spell ingredient allows you to link to the energy imbued in money that has circulated for years. You can find it for sale in many places online.

Combine all ingredients in a bottle during the waxing moon.

Abramelin Oil

Ingredients
- ½ teaspoon Cinnamon essential oil
- 1 ½ teaspoons Myrrh essential oil
- ½ teaspoon Galangal essential oil
- 2 tablespoons Olive Oil

This oil is used as a general altar and anointing oil for any magical or spiritual purpose. Abramelin oil is a classic anointing oil used in the Hermetic Order of the Golden Dawn, and by Thelemites, Pagans, and many other traditions. It comes from an old grimoire, *The Book of the Sacred Magic of Abramelin the Mage*. The text of this grimoire contains the date of 1458, but the earliest manuscript dates from 1608 and currently resides in Germany. The oil is an adaptation of an Abrahamic holy oil found in Jewish traditions and in the Bible (Exodus 30:22-25).

This recipe is based on the original Abramelin recipe, which was somewhat cryptic regarding ingredients. Specifically, there is considerable debate regarding the galangal root. The ingredient in the texts may have been calamus or another plant. This debate has been mostly resolved, and Aleister Crowley and other magicians prefer galangal root. Still, some Hermetic traditions continue to use calamus, and you can substitute calamus or another oil for the galangal if you desire.

Abramelin oil is traditionally made using olive oil. Because olive oil becomes rancid quickly, I make a concentrate using only the essential oils. When I need to refill my container of anointing oil, I mix 4 drops of the concentrate with 16 drops of olive oil. Use ½ teaspoon concentrate to a scant tablespoon of olive oil for larger bottles. You can add a few drops of vitamin E oil to the recipe to help prevent the olive oil from spoiling, but you should use any blends made with olive oil within three to four months.

Abramelin Oil Infusion

Ingredients
- 2 tablespoons crushed Myrrh resin
- ¼ cup Cinnamon chips
- 1 tablespoons Galangal Root chips or crushed slices
- ½ to 1 cup Olive Oil

This version uses spices and resins rather than essential oils and follows the original ratios from *The Book of the Sacred Magic of Abramelin the Mage.*

> *Take of myrrh in tears, one part; of fine cinnamon, two parts; of galangal half a part; and the half of the total weight of these drugs of the best oil olive. The which aromatics you shall mix together according unto the Art of the Apothecary, and shall make thereof a Balsam, the which you shall keep in a glass vial which you shall put within the cupboard (formed by the interior) of the Altar.*
> Translated by Samuel L. MacGregor Mathers, 1897

Fill a glass container with the myrrh, cinnamon, and galangal (or calamus if you prefer). Add olive oil to the container until it covers all of the botanicals. Allow this oil to age for several days before use. Store it in the refrigerator to increase its shelf life to about 18 months. If you use jojoba oil instead of the traditional olive oil, the shelf life increases to 3-4 years and you can store it at room temperature.

Black Cat Oil

Or Lucky Black Cat Oil

Ingredients
- ½ teaspoon Myrrh essential oil
- ½ teaspoon Clary Sage essential oil
- 1 teaspoon Bay Laurel essential oil
- 1 pinch Iron Filings – You can use a pinch of steel wool if you can't find iron filings.
- 3 tablespoons Base Oil

Black cat oil is traditionally used as an uncrossing oil to break hexes and curses. You can use it to anoint areas around the home to remove baneful influences and attract luck.

Ingredients
- 1 small magnet
- 3 whole coffee beans
- 1 pinch Rose Petals or 1 drop Rose Oil
- 1 drop Patchouli oil
- 1 pinch Cinnamon powder or 1 drop Cinnamon Oil
- 1 pinch Jasmine Flowers or 1 drop Jasmine Oil (If you cannot find jasmine flowers, you can use jasmine tea instead.)
- 2 pinches Lavender
- ½ to 2 ounces Base Oil

This traditional drawing oil should be created during the waxing moon phase. Come to me oil is normally used to compel someone you love to visit you or contact you. It is a lustful brew and you'll use it to anoint a red candle, and then apply a small amount just below your belly button.

Most Wiccans will never force their will upon others with this type of manipulation. However, this is an excellent and fast working oil that can be used for general attraction. Anoint a pink candle and apply some oil below your navel. Focus your intent on attracting a good partner and say words of power such as:

Come to me who is meant to be.
Let this cause no harm nor turn on me.

Or High John the Conqueror Root Oil

Ingredients
- 1 High John the Conqueror root
- 1 teaspoon Dragon's Blood resin – crushed into rice size pieces
- 2 teaspoons Cinnamon Chips
- ½ teaspoon Helichrysum Essential Oil

- 1 pinch Calendula Flower Petals
- 2 ounces Base Oil
- 1 Power Stone (optional) - such as Tiger Iron, Clear Quartz, Citrine, Carnelian, Garnet, Tiger's Eye, or Bloodstone

Combine all ingredients on a full or waxing moon. Sundays are good days to make this oil, and Tuesdays or Thursdays will also work. Refer to the monthly planner pages beginning on page 178 to find these auspicious times. High John the Conqueror root is also known as jalap root. It is the root of a type of morning glory and is used for power, confidence, love, courage, victory, money, virility, and luck. It helps to remove obstacles that prevent you from achieving your goals.

Pokeberry Ink

Pokeweed is surrounded by a great deal of folklore. It is associated with the planet Mars and magically corresponds to courage, hex-removal, and banishing.

The semi-toxic plant is used to make 'poke salad' but this requires boiling and several water changes to make it safe for consumption. The berries (pokeberries) are used to make dyes and inks. Pokeberry ink was used frequently in the United States during the 18th and 19th centuries, particularly during the Civil War.

To make pokeberry ink, harvest very ripe berries. Wearing gloves, smash the berries thoroughly and strain through several layers of cheesecloth or a flour sack towel.

Put the juice in a wide-mouth jar covered with a cloth and secured with a rubber band. Allow this jar to remain undisturbed for a week or two in a dark place (sunlight will turn your ink brown). As your juice sits it will ferment and some of the liquid will evaporate, leaving you with a more saturate color.

After a week or two, pour the juice through several layers of cheesecloth or a flour sack towel. Add one tablespoon of 70% to 95% isopropyl alcohol for every 4 ounces of juice to preserve your ink.

The result will be the perfect magical ink for dip pens that can be used like any of the other 'blood inks' used in magic such as bat's blood, dragon's blood, etc. Blood inks are used for writing spells, sigils, and runes. Pokeberry ink is especially known for its use in banishing.

Pokeberry ink is usually a dark fuchsia color. Over time, the dried ink will age to a dark reddish brown.

Making Moon Water

Moon water is water charged by the energy of the moon. It is usually made during the full moon, but you can use the power of any phase to charge your water. You can use moon water for many magical tasks:

- Use it to cleanse stones and altar tools.
- Put it in a spray bottle with a bit of lemon juice or vinegar for household cleansing and blessing.
- Use it to water your plants.
- Add it to lustral baths[10], or if you don't have a bathtub, you can pour moon water over your head as a final energy rinse.
- Use it to make tea, extracts, or ritual libations.
- Use it in the traditional dish for blessed water on your altar.

Directions

Fill a bowl, bottle, or jar with potable[11] water. For full and waxing moon water, place the container of water outside after sunset, where it will be exposed to direct moonlight. You might choose to say words of power and focus your intention when you set it out. Allow it to absorb the moon's energy for an hour or more, and remember to bring it back indoors before sunrise. For new and waning moon water, place your container out after sunrise[12] and continue as for full moon water, bringing it indoors before sunset.

---

10 A lustral bath is ritual bathing for purification before rituals.
11 Potable means suitable or safe for drinking.
12 The moon is overhead in the daytime during a new moon.

Do I Need to Protect Full Moon Water From Sunlight?

Usually, exposure of moon water to sunlight is discouraged. However, sunlight won't erase your intentions or the lunar energy already imbued into the water.

Can I Add Stones to My Moon Water?

Yes, with some caveats. Specific stones such as galena and malachite contain toxins that can leech into the water, making the moon water potentially toxic. Selenite and calcite can be damaged by prolonged contact with water. Stick with quartz crystals, amethyst, citrine, aventurine, moonstone, garnet, ruby, sapphire, aquamarine, and emerald.

Altar Incense

Altar incense is used for any spiritual or magical purpose. It promotes high vibrations and helps you enter into a magical mind set. It keeps baneful energies away and can be used for smoke cleansing. Parts in this recipe are by volume, so you can use a pinch, spoon, or measuring cup rather than a scale.

Ingredients
- 2 parts Frankincense resin
- 1 part Styrax resin
- 1 part White Copal or Copal Blanco resin
- 1 part Myrrh resin

Crush the resins into small, uniform sizes, about as big as a piece of rice. This is a traditional type of incense for use over incense charcoals. Do not use charcoals intended for barbecue grills as they emit toxic fumes. Only incense charcoals such as the one pictured here are suitable for indoor use.

Use a very small amount of this potent incense on your charcoal. Start with about ½ a teaspoon or the amount that easily fits inside the indentation in the charcoal.

Snickerdoodles

This is a variation on a classic cookie. They contain more cinnamon than the usual recipe, and chamomile is a unique ingredient. These ingredients correspond to love, money, comfort, and success.

1. Preheat oven to 350°F. If you are using a silicone, glass, or dark pan preheat to 325°F
2. In a large mixing bowl, whip together
   • **1 cup softened butter**
   • **1 ½ cups sugar**
3. When the butter and sugar are fluffy, whip in:
   • **2 large eggs**
   • **2 teaspoons vanilla extract**
4. Mix in
   • **2 ¾ cups flour**
   • **1 ½ teaspoons cream of tartar**
   • **½ teaspoon baking soda**
   • **1 teaspoon salt**
5. Wrap the dough and refrigerate for 1 hour. While waiting, make a finishing sugar mixture by combine the following:
   • **¼ cup sugar**
   • **1 tablespoon cinnamon**
   • **The contents of 1 chamomile tea bag – crushed fine in your mortar and pestle**

6. Remove dough from refrigerator and roll into small balls about 1 inch in diameter. Drop them into the finishing sugar mixture and gently roll them around until they are well coated. Place them on the cookie sheet (use parchment paper or nonstick spray) and press them very lightly to just slightly flatten the balls into disks.
7. Bake for 9-11 minutes. Leave them on the baking sheet for a few minutes to let them set up before removing.

Glossary

Abrahamic Religions

Religions that worship the God of Abraham including Judaism, Christianity, and Islam.

Apogee

(ăpʹə-jē) The point in the Moon's orbit when it is farthest away from earth. An easy way to remember this is **AP**ogee is means far **Ap**art.

Athame

Pronounce Ath-uh-may. A ritual knife, usually black handled with a double edged blade. Normally it is used ritually to direct energy or cut energetic bonds. It is not used to cut anything on the physical plane. The singular exception to this is that an athame is sometimes used to cut handfasting cakes. It can also be used for self defense on the astral plane.

Bane and Baneful

Bane is anything with an undesirable, contrary, or negative influence. It is a very relative term! Something can be baneful to certain people or in certain situations, while being a blessing for others or under different circumstances. Baneful magic is sometimes called black magic, however this dichotomy of good/evil – black/white – right/wrong, does not properly apply to magic and witchcraft as we tend to look beyond overly simplified and limiting binaries.

Besom

Pronounced bee-zum or bi-zəm, a besom is a broom, specifically a witch's broom that is used ritually to cleanse areas, for fertility rituals, and for handfasting. Handfasting rituals often involve "jumping the broom" and the bonded parties will jump over a besom to symbolize leaving their pasts behind and being united as they move forward into a new life.

Black Moon

There are three types of black moons. *1. A seasonal black moon* is the third new moon of an astronomical season in which there are four new moons. An astrological season is the time period between the quarter Sabbats (solstices and equinoxes). *2. A monthly black moon* is the second new moon in a calendar month with two new moons. *3. A February black moon* occurs about once every nineteen years. This is when there is either no full or no new moon during the month of February. Time zone differences mean that this last type of black moon is not necessarily a world-wide event.

Blue Moon

There are two types of blue moons. *1. A seasonal blue moon* is the third full Moon of an astronomical season in which there are four full Moons. An astrological season is the time period between the quarter Sabbats (solstices and equinoxes). *2. A monthly blue moon* is the second full Moon in a calendar month with two full moons.

Boline

Pronounced boh-leen. A ritual knife used for harvesting herbs, inscribing candles, cutting cords, and other practical ritual work. A boline often  has a white handle and occasionally has a crescent-shaped blade. Fancy designs with blades made of copper and silver can be found at witch shops, however I prefer a style of knife from Indonesia specifically developed for this type of work. This type of knife is known as a *karambit* (pictured) and maintains the crescent or claw shape, but won't damage plants when pruning or harvesting, and the steel takes a sharper edge.

Book of Shadows (bos)

A combination of journal, scrapbook, spells, rituals, recipes, and correspondences. Many witches keep a bos, either printed or digitally. They are very useful for keeping track of experiments and for developing your personal path.

Cast Lots or Draw Lots

Casting lots refers to making a random selection. When cards are used it is usually referred to as drawing lots, a form of cartomancy. When runes, bones, shells, grain, coins, or other tools of cleromancy are used it is normally referred to as casting lots.

Cauldron

Traditionally a cauldron is a cast-iron pot. Iron has protective energy and the heat-proof pot works well as a censer. Three-legged pots are favorites for witches because the number three can represent the three phases of the Goddess, the three-fold law, or the phases of the moon.

Cense & Censing

A very old term for smoke-cleansing, meaning to perfume with incense, or to infuse something with incense smoke. This term is preferred over the culturally appropriated word *smudging*.

Censer

An incense burner or thurible.

Conjunction

The time at which a planet appears closest to the sun as seen from earth.

Deosil

Clockwise movement, also known as sun-wise.

Divination

Gaining insight through spiritual means such as scrying, tarot cards, runes, tea leaves, or other methods.

Doctrine of Signatures

An ancient concept that plants resemble the body part for which they can be used to heal.

Esbat

A ritual held on full moons, sometimes also on new moons.

Exact Cross-Quarters

The precise half-way point between a solstice and an equinox as measured along the ecliptic. Also known as Astronomical Cross-Quarters.

Handfasting

A type of bonding ritual somewhat similar to a marriage. The spiritual bond is agreed upon by all parties involved, and often includes a set time period. Many choose to handfast for "a year and a day". When that period of time comes to an end, those involved review the relationship and decide to either renew their handfasting or go their separate ways. Handfasting can also be "until death do us part" or "for now and all of eternity".

Manifest and Manifestation

Made popular by the book and film The Secret, these terms are commonly used in reference to the focusing of one's thoughts upon a desired outcome. Witches have adopted the term as a way to quickly express the focusing of our energy, will, and intent to create change in the physical world or within ourselves. Manifestation can also refer to spiritual forms or entities appearing in the physical world, however in this instance the term materialization is better suited.

Micro Moon

A new or full Moon that occurs during apogee. The moon is farther away and may appear smaller.

Mountweazel

A person who claims the work and research of other witches as their own, or copies and distributes the work of others without permission. Formerly known as a cowan.

Opposition

The time at which a planet appears opposite the sun as seen from earth.

Perigee

(pĕr′ə-jē) The point in the Moon's orbit when it is closest to earth. Peri comes from the Greek word for *near*.

Poppet

A poppet is a figure or doll fashioned to resemble a person who is the target of a spell. The Law of Similarity is evident because the poppet is made to look like the target of a spell. The Law of Contagion is often employed by incorporating hair or other items from the target into the doll.

Power Hand

Some practitioners prefer to use one hand for sensing and receiving energy, and the other hand for sending or projecting. The sending hand is your power hand, and it is often the dominant hand or the one you write with.

Querent

The person who seeks information from an oracle or divination. Sometimes referred to as *the client* or *the questioner*.

Sabbats

Major festivals, celebrations, and/or holy days celebrated by Witches and many modern Pagans. There are eight Sabbats, the two solstices and two equinoxes (Quarters), and the midpoints in the year between them (Cross-Quarters). The names used for each of the Sabbats, and the number celebrated, vary by tradition.

So mote it be

Frequently incorporated into words of power or used at the end of a spell to "seal and send". It means *let it be so, so shall it be,* or *it is so.*

Spell Bag

Sometimes called a mojo bag or conjure pouch. A spell bag is a type of talisman filled with a variety of items such as stones, herbs, and charms. Like the popular spell jar, spell bags are designed for specific purposes. The color of the bag is traditionally red, but modern witches choose other colors to coincide with the purpose, such as green for luck or money.

Super Moon

A new or full Moon that occurs during perigee. The Moon is close to earth and may appear larger and brighter.

Syncretic

Combining different philosophical, religious, or cultural prin-ciples and practices. For example, a Witch might combine Western occultism with ancient folk traditions, neo-Pagan practices, and modern science.

Three-fold Law

Also known as the law of three.

Thurible

An incense burner or censer. Thuribles are often made of perforated metal such as brass and hung from chains.

Vernal

As in Vernal Equinox Sabbat. Vernal means spring in reference to the season.

Widdershins

Counter-clockwise movement

Words of Power

Words of power are the words used in spells or rituals that are spoken or chanted with a resounding tone to carry your energy out into the universe. They often rhyme to make them easier to memorize and so they resonate harmoniously.

Wortcunning

Wortcunning is the knowledge of the magical and medicinal properties of botanicals, the understanding of how to use these natural materials, and the wisdom of knowing when and why to use them. "Wort" refers to plants, and cunning refers to cleverness and skill.

Index

Index

About the Author

Friday Gladheart founded the first online academy for witch-craft, tarot, and magical herbalism in 1996. She remains an instructor at WitchAcademy.org and produces the *Practical Witch Talk* podcast. For over 35 years she has been a professional tarot reader, and continues to do tarot readings on weekends. The rest of her time is spent developing an organic teaching garden and Pagan sanctuary near the Ouachita National Forest. Herbs from the sanctuary are incorporated into many of the products she makes for the Practical Witch Shop. Her incense and tea varieties can be found in shops worldwide.

Please stay in touch! Visit PracticalWitch.com to sign up for the newsletter. You'll get more great articles, event updates, and bonus materials with every newsletter.

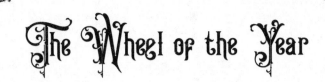

The Wheel of the Year

The annual cycle of Sabbats is the Wheel of the Year. The Wheel changes slightly every year due to the shifting dates of the solstices and equinoxes.

If you color the Wheel of the Year below I'd love to see it! Tag me on Instagram @Practical.Witches or on Facebook @PracticalWitch.

MICROCOSM · PUBLISHING

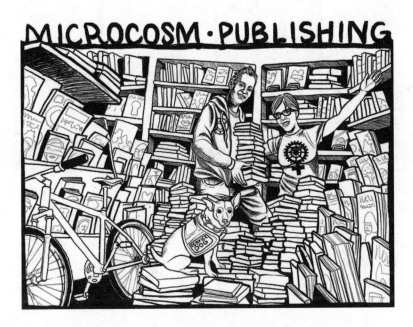

About the Publisher

MICROCOSM PUBLISHING is Portland's most diversified publishing house and distributor with a focus on the colorful, authentic, and empowering. Our books and zines have put your power in your hands since 1996, equipping readers to make positive changes in their lives and in the world around them. Microcosm emphasizes skill-building, showing hidden histories, and fostering creativity through challenging conventional publishing wisdom with books and bookettes about DIY skills, food, bicycling, gender, self-care, and social justice. What was once a distro and record label started by Joe Biel in a drafty bedroom was determined to be *Publisher's Weekly's* fastest growing publisher of 2022 and has become among the oldest independent publishing houses in Portland, OR and Cleveland, OH. We are a politically moderate, centrist publisher in a world that has inched to the right for the past 80 years.

Global labor conditions are bad, and our roots in industrial Cleveland in the 70s and 80s made us appreciate the need to treat workers right. Therefore, our books are MADE IN THE USA

Did you know that you can buy our books directly from us at sliding scale rates? Support a small, independent publisher and pay less than Amazon's price at **www. Microcosm.Pub**